10418

Date Due

Oct 9 —			
Oct 30			
9-30-85			
11-4-85			
9-12-90			
3-8-93			
3/29/95			

D1126578

PIONEERS OF THE OLD SOUTHWEST

EXTRA-ILLUSTRATED EDITION

∵

VOLUME 18
THE CHRONICLES
OF AMERICA SERIES
ALLEN JOHNSON
EDITOR

GERHARD R. LOMER
CHARLES W. JEFFERYS
ASSISTANT EDITORS

DANIEL BOONE

Old engraving after a painting by Chester Harding. Photograph in the collections of Archibald Henderson, Chapel Hill, N. C.

DANIEL BOONE

Old engraving after a painting by Chester Harding. Photograph in
the collections of Archibald Henderson, Chapel Hill, N. C.

PIONEERS OF THE OLD SOUTHWEST

A CHRONICLE OF THE
DARK AND BLOODY GROUND
BY CONSTANCE LINDSAY SKINNER

NEW HAVEN: YALE UNIVERSITY PRESS
TORONTO: GLASGOW, BROOK & CO.
LONDON: HUMPHREY MILFORD
OXFORD UNIVERSITY PRESS

1920

ACKNOWLEDGMENT

THIS narrative is founded largely on original sources—on the writings and journals of pioneers and contemporary observers, such as Doddridge and Adair, and on the public documents of the period as printed in the Colonial Records and in the American Archives. But the author is, nevertheless, greatly indebted to the researches of other writers, whose works are cited in the Bibliographical Note. The author's thanks are due, also, to Dr. Archibald Henderson, of the University of North Carolina, for his kindness in reading the proofs of this book for comparison with his own extended collection of unpublished manuscripts relating to the period.

C. L. S.

April, 1919.

CONTENTS

ILLUSTRATIONS

PIONEERS OF THE OLD SOUTHWEST

∵

CHAPTER I

THE TREAD OF PIONEERS

THE Ulster Presbyterians, or "Scotch-Irish," to whom history has ascribed the dominant rôle among the pioneer folk of the Old Southwest, began their migrations to America in the latter years of the seventeenth century. It is not known with certainty precisely when or where the first immigrants of their race arrived in this country, but soon after 1680 they were to be found in several of the colonies. It was not long, indeed, before they were entering in numbers at the port of Philadelphia and were making Pennsylvania the chief center of their activities in the New World. By 1726 they had established settlements in several counties behind Philadelphia. Ten years later they had begun their great trek southward through

1

the Shenandoah Valley of Virginia and on to the Yadkin Valley of North Carolina. There they met others of their own race — bold men like themselves, hungry after land — who were coming in through Charleston and pushing their way up the rivers from the seacoast to the "Back Country," in search of homes.

These Ulstermen did not come to the New World as novices in the shaping of society; they had already made history. Their ostensible object in America was to obtain land, but, like most external aims, it was secondary to a deeper purpose. What had sent the Ulstermen to America was a passion for a whole freedom. They were lusty men, shrewd and courageous, zealous to the death for an ideal and withal so practical to the moment in business that it soon came to be commonly reported of them that "they kept the Sabbath and everything else they could lay their hands on," though it is but fair to them to add that this phrase is current wherever Scots dwell. They had contested in Parliament and with arms for their own form of worship and for their civil rights. They were already frontiersmen, trained in the hardihood and craft of border warfare through years of guerrilla fighting with the Irish Celts. They had pitted and proved their strength against a wilderness; they had reclaimed the North of Ireland from desolation. For the time, many of them were educated men; under the regulations of the Presbyterian Church every child was taught to read at an early age, since no person could be admitted to the privileges of the Church who did not both understand and approve the Presbyterian constitution and discipline. They were brought up on the Bible and on the writings of their famous pastors, one of whom, as early as 1650, had given utterance to the democratic doctrine that "men are called to the magistracy by the suffrage of the people whom they govern, and for men to assume unto themselves power is mere tyranny and unjust usurpation." In subscribing to this doctrine and in resisting to the hilt all efforts of successive English kings to interfere in the election of their pastors, the Scots of Ulster had already declared for democracy.

It was shortly after James VI of Scotland became James I of England and while the English were founding Jamestown that the Scots had first occupied Ulster; but the true origin of the Ulster Plantation lies further back, in the reign of Henry VIII, in the days of the English Reformation. In Henry's Irish realm the Reformation, though proclaimed by royal authority, had never been accomplished; and Henry's more famous daughter, Elizabeth, had conceived the plan, later to be carried out by James, of planting colonies of Protestants in Ireland to promote loyalty in that rebellious land. Six counties, comprising half a million acres, formed the Ulster Plantation. The great majority of the colonists sent thither by James were Scotch Lowlanders, but among them were many English and a smaller number of Highlanders. These three peoples from the island of Britain brought forth, through intermarriage, the Ulster Scots.

The reign of Charles I had inaugurated for the Ulstermen an era of persecution. Charles practically suppressed the Presbyterian religion in Ireland. His son, Charles II, struck at Ireland in 1666 through its cattle trade, by prohibiting the exportation of beef to England and Scotland. The Navigation Acts, excluding Ireland from direct trade with the colonies, ruined Irish commerce, while Corporation Acts and Test Acts requiring conformity with the practices of the Church of England bore heavily on the Ulster Presbyterians.

It was largely by refugees from religious persecution that America in the beginning was colonized. But religious persecution was only one of the influences which shaped the course and formed the character of the Ulster Scots. In Ulster, whither they had originally been transplanted by James to found a loyal province in the midst of the King's enemies, they had done their work too well and had waxed too powerful for the comfort of later monarchs. The first attacks upon them struck at their religion; but the subsequent legislative acts which successively ruined the woolen trade, barred nonconformists from public office, stifled Irish commerce, pronounced non-Episcopal marriages irregular, and instituted heavy taxation and high rentals for the land their fathers had made productive—these were blows dealt chiefly for the political and commercial ends of favored classes in England.

These attacks, aimed through his religious conscience at the sources of his livelihood, made the Ulster Scot perforce what he was — a zealot as a citizen and a zealot as a merchant no less than as a Presbyterian. Thanks to his persecutors, he made a religion of everything he undertook and regarded his civil rights as divine rights. Thus out of persecution emerged a type of man who was high-principled and narrow, strong and violent, as tenacious of his own rights as he was blind often to the rights of others, acquisitive yet self-sacrificing, but most of all fearless, confident of his own power, determined to have and to hold.

Twenty thousand Ulstermen, it is estimated, left Ireland for America in the first three decades of the eighteenth century. More than six thousand of them are known to have entered Pennsylvania in 1729 alone, and twenty years later they numbered one-quarter of that colony's population. During the five years preceding the Revolutionary War more than thirty thousand Ulstermen crossed the ocean and arrived in America just in time and in just the right frame of mind to return King George's compliment in kind, by helping to deprive him of his American estates, a domain very much larger than the acres of Ulster. They fully justified the fears of the good bishop who wrote Lord Dartmouth, Secretary for the Colonies, that he trembled for the peace of the King's overseas realm, since these thousands of "phanatical and hungry Republicans" had sailed for America.

The Ulstermen who entered by Charleston were known to the inhabitants of the tidewater regions as the "Scotch-Irish." Those who came from the north, lured southward by the offer of cheap lands, were called the "Pennsylvania Irish." Both were, however, of the same race — a race twice expatriated, first from Scotland and then from Ireland, and stripped of all that it had won throughout more than a century of persecution. To these exiles the Back Country of North Carolina, with its cheap and even free tracts lying far from the seat of government, must have seemed not only the Land of Promise but the Land of Last Chance. Here they must strike their roots into the sod with such interlocking strength that no cataclysm of tyranny should ever dislodge them — or they must accept the fate dealt out to them by their former persecutors and become a tribe of nomads and serfs. But to these Ulster immigrants such a choice was no choice at all. They knew themselves strong men, who had made the most of opportunity despite almost superhuman obstacles. The drumming of their feet along the banks of the Shenandoah, or up the rivers from Charleston, and on through the broad sweep of the Yadkin Valley, was a conquering people's challenge to the Wilderness which lay sleeping like an unready sentinel at the gates of their Future.

It is maintained still by many, however often disputed, that the Ulstermen were the first to declare for American Independence, as in the Old Country they were the first to demand the separation of

Church and State. A Declaration of Independence is said to have been drawn up and signed in Mecklenburg County, North Carolina, on May 20, 1775.[1] However that may be, it is certain that these Mecklenburg Protestants had received special schooling in the doctrine of independence. They had in their midst for eight years (1758–66) the Reverend Alexander Craighead, a Presbyterian minister who, for his "republican doctrines" expressed in a pamphlet, had been disowned by the Pennsylvania Synod acting on the Governor's protest, and so persecuted in Virginia that he had at last fled to the North Carolina Back Country. There, during the remaining years of his life, as the sole preacher and teacher in the settlements between the Yadkin and the Catawba rivers he found willing soil in which to sow the seeds of Liberty.

There was another branch of the Scottish race which helped to people the Back Country. The Highlanders, whose loyalty to their oath made them fight on the King's side in the Revolutionary War, have been somewhat overlooked in history. Tradition, handed down among the transplanted

[1] See Hoyt, *The Mecklenburg Declaration of Independence;* and *American Archives*, Fourth Series, vol. ii, p. 855.

clans — who, for the most part, spoke only Gaelic for a generation and wrote nothing — and latterly recorded by one or two of their descendants, supplies us with all we are now able to learn of the early coming of the Gaels to Carolina. It would seem that their first immigration to America in small bands took place after the suppression of the Jacobite rising in 1715 — when Highlanders fled in numbers also to France — for by 1729 there was a settlement of them on the Cape Fear River. We know, too, that in 1748 it was charged against Gabriel Johnston, Governor of North Carolina from 1734 to 1752, that he had shown no joy over the King's "glorious victory of Culloden" and that "he had appointed one William McGregor, who had been in the Rebellion in the year 1715 a Justice of the Peace during the last Rebellion [1745] and was not himself without suspicion of disaffection to His Majesty's Government." It is indeed possible that Gabriel Johnston, formerly a professor at St. Andrew's University, had himself not always been a stranger to the kilt. He induced large numbers of Highlanders to come to America and probably influenced the second George to moderate his treatment of the vanquished Gaels in the Old Country and permit their emigration to the New World.

In contrast with the Ulstermen, whose secular ideals were dictated by the forms of their Church, these Scots adhered still to the tribal or clan system, although they, too, in the majority, were Presbyterians, with a minority of Roman Catholics and Episcopalians.   In the Scotch Highlands they had occupied small holdings on the land under the sway of their chief, or Head of the Clan, to whom they were bound by blood and fealty but to whom they paid no rentals. The position of the Head of the Clan was hereditary, but no heir was bold enough to step forward into that position until he had performed some deed of worth. They were principally herders, their chief stock being the famous small black cattle of the Highlands. Their wars with each other were cattle raids. Only in war, however, did the Gael lay hands on his neighbor's goods. There were no highwaymen and housebreakers in the Highlands. No Highland mansion, cot, or barn was ever locked. Theft and the breaking of an oath, sins against man's honor, were held in such abhorrence that no one guilty of them could remain among his clansmen in the beloved glens. These Highlanders were a race of tall, robust men, who lived simply and frugally and slept on the heath among their flocks in all weathers, with no other covering from rain and snow than their plaidies. It is reported of the Laird of Keppoch, who was leading his clan to war in winter time, that his men were divided as to the propriety of following him further because he rolled a snowball to rest his head upon when he lay down. "Now we despair of victory," they said, "since our leader has become so effeminate he cannot sleep without a pillow!"[1]

The "King's glorious victory of Culloden" was followed by a policy of extermination carried on by the orders and under the personal direction of the Duke of Cumberland. When King George at last restrained his son from his orgy of blood, he offered the Gaels their lives and exile to America on condition of their taking the full oath of allegiance. The majority accepted his terms, for not only were their lives forfeit but their crops and cattle had been destroyed and the holdings on which their ancestors had lived for many centuries taken from them. The descriptions of the scenes attending their leave-taking of the hills and glens they loved with such passionate fervor are among the most pathetic in history. Strong men who had met the ravage of a brutal sword without weakening

[1] MacLean, *An Historical Account of the Settlement of Scotch Highlanders in America.*

abandoned themselves to the agony of sorrow.
They kissed the walls of their houses. They flung
themselves on the ground and embraced the sod
upon which they had walked in freedom. They
called their broken farewells to the peaks and lochs
of the land they were never again to see; and, as
they turned their backs and filed down through the
passes, their pipers played the dirge for the dead.

Such was the character, such the deep feeling,
of the race which entered North Carolina from the
coast and pushed up into the wilderness about the
headwaters of Cape Fear River. Tradition indi-
cates that these hillsmen sought the interior because the grass and pea vine which overgrew the
inner country stretching towards the mountains provided excellent fodder for the cattle which some of
the chiefs are said to have brought with them.
These Gaelic herders, perhaps in negligible numbers, were in the Yadkin Valley before 1730, possibly even ten years earlier. In 1739 Neil MacNeill
of Kintyre brought over a shipload of Gaels to
rejoin his kinsman, Hector MacNeill, called Bluff
Hector from his residence near the bluffs at Cross
Creek, now Fayetteville. Some of these immigrants
went on to the Yadkin, we are told, to unite with
others of their clan who had been for some time in

that district. The exact time of the first Highlander on the Yadkin cannot be ascertained, as
there were no court records and the offices of the
land companies were not then open for the sale
of these remote regions. But by 1753 there were
not less than four thousand Gaels in Cumberland
County, where they occupied the chief magisterial
posts; and they were already spreading over the
lands now comprised within Moore, Anson, Richmond, Robeson, Bladen, and Sampson counties.
In these counties Gaelic was as commonly heard
as English.

In the years immediately preceding the Revolution and even in 1776 itself they came in increasing
numbers. They knew nothing of the smoldering
fire just about to break into flames in the country
of their choice, but the Royal Governor, Josiah
Martin, knew that Highland arms would soon be
needed by His Majesty. He knew something of
Highland honor, too; for he would not let the
Gaels proceed after their landing until they had
bound themselves by oath to support the Government of King George. So it was that the unfortunate Highlanders found themselves, according
to their strict code of honor, forced to wield arms
against the very Americans who had received and

befriended them — and for the crowned brother of a prince whose name is execrated to this day in Highland song and story!

They were led by Allan MacDonald of Kingsborough; and tradition gives us a stirring picture of Allan's wife — the famous Flora MacDonald, who in Scotland had protected the Young Pretender in his flight—making an impassioned address in Gaelic to the Highland soldiers and urging them on to die for honor's sake. When this Highland force was conquered by the Americans, the large majority willingly bound themselves not to fight further against the American cause and were set at liberty. Many of them felt that, by offering their lives to the swords of the Americans, they had canceled their obligation to King George and were now free to draw their swords again and, this time, in accordance with their sympathies; so they went over to the American side and fought gallantly for independence.

Although the brave glory of this pioneer age shines so brightly on the Lion Rampant of Caledonia, not to Scots alone does that whole glory belong. The second largest racial stream which flowed into the Back Country of Virginia and

North Carolina was German. Most of these Germans went down from Pennsylvania and were generally called "Pennsylvania Dutch," an incorrect rendering of *Pennsylvänische Deutsche*. The upper Shenandoah Valley was settled almost entirely by Germans. They were members of the Lutheran, German Reformed, and Moravian churches. The cause which sent vast numbers of this sturdy people across the ocean, during the first dozen years of the eighteenth century, was religious persecution. By statute and by sword the Roman Catholic powers of Austria sought to wipe out the Salzburg Lutherans and the Moravian followers of John Huss. In that region of the Rhine country known in those days as the German Palatinate, now a part of Bavaria, Protestants were being massacred by the troops of Louis of France, then engaged in the War of the Spanish Succession (1701–13) and in the zealous effort to extirpate heretics from the soil of Europe. In 1708, by proclamation, Good Queen Anne offered protection to the persecuted Palatines and invited them to her dominions. Twelve thousand of them went to England, where they were warmly received by the English. But it was no slight task to settle twelve thousand immigrants of an alien speech in

England and enable them to become independent and self-supporting. A better solution of their problem lay in the Western World. The Germans needed homes and the Queen's overseas dominions needed colonists. They were settled at first along the Hudson, and eventually many of them took up lands in the fertile valley of the Mohawk.

For fifty years or more German and Austrian Protestants poured into America. In Pennsylvania their influx averaged about fifteen hundred a year, and that colony became the distributing center for the German race in America. By 1727, Adam Müller and his little company had established the first white settlement in the Valley of Virginia. In 1732 Joist Heydt went south from York, Pennsylvania, and settled on the Opequan Creek at or near the site of the present city of Winchester.

The life of Count Zinzendorf, called "the Apostle," one of the leaders of the Moravian immigrants, glows like a star out of those dark and troublous times. Of high birth and gentle nurture, he forsook whatever of ease his station promised him and fitted himself for evangelical work. In 1741 he visited the Wyoming Valley to bring his religion to the Delawares and Shawanoes. He was not of those picturesque Captains of the Lord who

bore their muskets on their shoulders when they
went forth to preach. Armored only with the
shield of faith, the helmet of salvation, and the
sword of the spirit, his feet "shod with the preparation of the gospel of peace," he went out into the
country of these bloodthirsty tribes and told them
that he had come to them in their darkness to
teach the love of the Christ which lighteth the
world. The Indians received him suspiciously.
One day while he sat in his tent writing, some
Delawares drew near to slay him and were about
to strike when they saw two deadly snakes crawl
in from the opposite side of the tent, move directly
towards the Apostle, and pass harmlessly over his
body. Thereafter they regarded him as under
spiritual protection. Indeed so widespread was
his good fame among the tribes that for some years
all Moravian settlements along the borders were
unmolested. Painted savages passed through on
their way to war with enemy bands or to raid the
border, but for the sake of one consecrated spirit,
whom they had seen death avoid, they spared
the lives and goods of his fellow believers. When
Zinzendorf departed a year later, his mantle fell
on David Zeisberger, who lived the love he taught
for over fifty years and converted many savages.

Zeisberger was taken before the Governor and army heads at Philadelphia, who had only too good reason to be suspicious of priestly counsels in the tents of Shem: but he was able to impress white men no less than simple savages with the nobility of the doctrine he had learned from the Apostle.

In 1751 the Moravian Brotherhood purchased one hundred thousand acres in North Carolina from Lord Granville. Bishop Spangenburg was commissioned to survey this large acreage, which was situated in the present county of Forsyth east of the Yadkin, and which is historically listed as the Wachovia Tract. In 1753, twelve Brethren left the Moravian settlements of Bethlehem and Nazareth, in Pennsylvania, and journeyed southward to begin the founding of a colony on their new land. Brother Adam Grube, one of the twelve, kept a diary of the events of this expedition.[1]

Honor to whom honor is due. We have paid it, in some measure, to the primitive Gaels of the Highlands for their warrior strength and their fealty, and to the enlightened Scots of Ulster for their enterprise and for their sacrifice unto blood that free conscience and just laws might promote the

[1] This diary is printed in full in *Travels in the American Colonies*. edited by N. D. Mereness.

progress and safeguard the intercourse of their
kind. Now let us take up for a moment Brother
Grube's *Journal* even as we welcome, perhaps the
more gratefully, the mild light of evening after the
flooding sun, or as our hearts, when too strongly
stirred by the deeds of men, turn for rest to the
serene faith and the naïve speech of little children.

The twelve, we learn, were under the leadership
of one of their number, Brother Gottlob. Their
earliest alarms on the march were not caused, as
we might expect, by anticipations of the painted
Cherokee, but by encounters with the strenuous
"Irish." One of these came and laid himself to
sleep beside the Brethren's camp fire on their first
night out, after they had sung their evening hymn
and eleven had stretched themselves on the earth
for slumber, while Brother Gottlob, their leader,
hanging his hammock between two trees, ascended — not only in spirit — a little higher than his
charges, and "rested well in it." Though the alarming Irishman did not disturb them, the Brethren's
doubts of that race continued, for Brother Grube
wrote on the 14th of October: "About four in the
morning we set up our tent, going four miles
beyond Carl Isles [Carlisle, seventeen miles southwest of Harrisburg] so as not to be too near the

Irish Presbyterians. After breakfast the Brethren shaved and then we rested under our tent. . . . People who were staying at the Tavern came to see what kind of folk we were. . . . Br Gottlob held the evening service and then we lay down around our cheerful fire, and Br Gottlob in his hammock." Two other jottings give us a racial kaleidoscope of the settlers and wayfarers of that time. On one day the Brethren bought "some hay from a Swiss," later "some kraut from a German which tasted very good to us"; and presently "an Englishman came by and drank a cup of tea with us and was very grateful for it." Frequently the little band paused while some of the Brethren went off to the farms along the route to help "cut hay." These kindly acts were usually repaid with gifts of food or produce.

One day while on the march they halted at a tavern and farm in Shenandoah Valley kept by a man whose name Brother Grube wrote down as "Severe." Since we know that Brother Grube's spelling of names other than German requires editing, we venture to hazard a guess that the name he attempted to set down as it sounded to him was Sevier. And we wonder if, in his brief sojourn, he saw a lad of eight years, slim, tall, and blond, with daring and mischievous blue eyes, and a certain curve of the lips that threatened havoc in the hearts of both sexes when he should be a man and reach out with swift hands and reckless will for his desires. If he saw this lad, he beheld John Sevier, later to become one of the most picturesque and beloved heroes of the Old Southwest.

Hardships abounded on the Brethren's journey, but faith and the Christian's joy, which no man taketh from him, met and surmounted them. "Three and a half miles beyond, the road forked. . . . We took the right hand road but found no water for ten miles. It grew late and we had to drive five miles into the night to find a stopping-place." Two of the Brethren went ahead "to seek out the road" through the darkened wilderness. There were rough hills in the way; and, the horses being exhausted, "Brethren had to help push." But, in due season, "Br Nathanael held evening prayer and then we slept in the care of Jesus," with Brother Gottlob as usual in his hammock. Three days later the record runs: "Toward evening we saw Jeams River, the road to it ran down so very steep a hill that we fastened a small tree to the back of our wagon, locked the wheels, and the Brethren held back by the tree with all their might." Even then the wagon went down so fast that most of the Brethren lost their footing and rolled and tumbled pell-mell. But Faith makes little of such mishaps: "No harm was done and we thanked the Lord that he had so graciously protected us, for it looked dangerous and we thought at times that it could not possibly be done without accident but we got down safely . . . we were all very tired and sleepy and let the angels be our guard during the night." Rains fell in torrents, making streams almost impassable and drenching the little band to the skin. The hammock was empty one night, for they had to spend the dark hours trench-digging about their tent to keep it from being washed away. Two days later (the 10th of November) the weather cleared and "we spent most of the day drying our blankets and mending and darning our stockings." They also bought supplies from settlers who, as Brother Grube observed without irony,

are glad we have to remain here so long and that it means money for them. In the afternoon we held a little Lovefeast and rested our souls in the loving sacrifice of Jesus, wishing for beloved Brethren in Bethlehem and that they and we might live ever close to Him. . . . Nov. 16. We rose early to ford the river. The bank was so steep that we hung a tree behind the wagon, fastening it in such a way that we could quickly release it when the wagon reached the water. The current was very swift and the lead horses were carried down a bit with it. The water just missed running into the wagon but we came safely to the other bank, which however we could not climb but had to take half the things out of the wagon, tie ropes to the axle on which we could pull, help our horses which were quite stiff, and so we brought our ark again to dry land.

On the evening of the 17th of November the twelve arrived safely on their land on the "Etkin" (Yadkin), having been six weeks on the march. They found with joy that, as ever, the Lord had provided for them. This time the gift was a deserted cabin, "large enough that we could all lie down around the walls. We at once made preparation for a little Lovefeast and rejoiced heartily with one another."

In the deserted log cabin, which, to their faith, seemed as one of those mansions "not built with hands" and descended miraculously from the heavens, they held their Lovefeast, while wolves padded and howled about the walls; and in that Pentacostal hour the tongue of fire descended upon Brother Gottlob, so that he made a new song unto the Lord. Who shall venture to say it is not better worth preserving than many a classic?

We hold arrival Lovefeast here
  In Carolina land,
A company of Brethren true,
  A little Pilgrim-Band,
Called by the Lord to be of those
  Who through the whole world go,
To bear Him witness everywhere
  And nought but Jesus know.

Then, we are told, the Brethren lay down to rest
and "*Br Gottlob hung his hammock above our heads*"
— as was most fitting on this of all nights; for is
not the Poet's place always just a little nearer to
the stars?

The pioneers did not always travel in groups.
There were families who set off alone. One of these
now claims our attention, for there was a lad in this
family whose name and deeds were to sound like
a ballad of romance from out the dusty pages of
history. This family's name was Boone.

Neither Scots nor Germans can claim Daniel
Boone; he was in blood a blend of English and
Welsh; in character wholly English. His grandfather George Boone was born in 1666 in the hamlet of Stoak, near Exeter in Devonshire. George
Boone was a weaver by trade and a Quaker by
religion. In England in his time the Quakers were

oppressed, and George Boone therefore sought information of William Penn, his coreligionist, regarding the colony which Penn had established in
America. In 1712 he sent his three elder children,
George, Sarah, and Squire, to spy out the land.
Sarah and Squire remained in Pennsylvania, while
their brother returned to England with glowing reports. On August 17, 1717, George Boone, his wife,
and the rest of his children journeyed to Bristol and
sailed for Philadelphia, arriving there on the 10th
of October. The Boones went first to Abingdon,
the Quaker farmers' community. Later they moved
to the northwestern frontier hamlet of North Wales,
a Welsh community which, a few years previously,
had turned Quaker. Sarah Boone married a German named Jacob Stover, who had settled in Oley
Township, Berks County. In 1718 George Boone
took up four hundred acres in Oley, or, to be exact,
in the subdivision later called Exeter, and there he
lived in his log cabin until 1744, when he died at
the age of seventy-eight. He left eight children,
fifty-two grandchildren, and ten great-grandchil-
dren, seventy descendants in all — English, German, Welsh, and Scotch-Irish blended into one
family of Americans.[1]

[1] R. G. Thwaites, *Daniel Boone*, p. 5.

Among the Welsh Quakers was a family of Morgans. In 1720 Squire Boone married Sarah Morgan. Ten years later he obtained 250 acres in Oley on Owatin Creek, eight miles southeast of the present city of Reading; and here, in 1734, Daniel Boone was born, the fourth son and sixth child of Squire and Sarah Morgan Boone. Daniel Boone therefore was a son of the frontier. In his childhood he became familiar with hunters and with Indians, for even the red men came often in friendly fashion to his grandfather's house. Squire Boone enlarged his farm by thrift. He continued at his trade of weaving and kept five or six looms going, making homespun cloth for the market and his neighbors.

Daniel's father owned grazing grounds several miles north of the homestead and each season he sent his stock to the range. Sarah Boone and her little Daniel drove the cows. From early spring till late autumn, mother and son lived in a rustic cabin alone on the frontier. A rude dairy house stood over a cool spring, and here Sarah Boone made her butter and cheese. Daniel, aged ten at this time, watched the herds; at sunset he drove them to the cabin for milking, and locked them in the cowpens at night.

He was not allowed firearms at that age, so he shaped for himself a weapon that served him well. This was a slender smoothly shaved sapling with a small bunch of gnarled roots at one end. So expert was he in the launching of this primitive spear that he easily brought down birds and small game. When he reached his twelfth year, his father bought him a rifle; and he soon became a crack shot. A year later we find him setting off on the autumn hunt — after driving the cattle in for the winter — with all the keenness and courage of a man twice his thirteen years. His rifle enabled him to return with meat for the family and skins to be traded in Philadelphia. When he was fourteen his brother Sam married Sarah Day, an intelligent young Quakeress who took a special interest in her young brother-in-law and taught him "the rudiments of three R's."

The Boones were prosperous and happy in Oley and it may be wondered why they left their farms and their looms, both of which were profitable, and set their faces towards the Unknown. It is recorded that, though the Boones were Quakers, they were of a high mettle and were not infrequently dealt with by the Meeting. Two of Squire Boone's children married "worldlings" — non-Quakers — and

were in consequence "disowned" by the Society.
In defiance of his sect, which strove to make him
sever all connection with his unruly offspring,
Squire Boone refused to shut his doors on the
son and the daughter who had scandalized local
Quakerdom. The Society of Friends thereupon expelled him. This occurred apparently during the
winter of 1748–49. In the spring of 1750 we see
the whole Boone family (save two sons) with their
wives and children, their household goods and
their stock, on the great highway, bound for a land
where the hot heart and the belligerent spirit shall
not be held amiss.

Southward through the Shenandoah goes the
Boone caravan. The women and children usually
sit in the wagons. The men march ahead or alongside, keeping a keen eye open for Indian or other
enemy in the wild, their rifles under arm or over
the shoulder. Squire Boone, who has done with
Quakerdom and is leading all that he holds dear
out to larger horizons, is ahead of the line, as we
picture him, ready to meet first whatever danger
may assail his tribe. He is a strong wiry man of
rather small stature, with ruddy complexion, red
hair, and gray eyes. Somewhere in the line, together, we think, are the mother and son who have

herded cattle and companioned each other through long months in the cabin on the frontier. We do not think of this woman as riding in the wagon, though she may have done so, but prefer to picture her, with her tall robust body, her black hair, and her black eyes — with the sudden Welsh snap in them — walking as sturdily as any of her sons.

If Daniel be beside her, what does she see when she looks at him? A lad well set up but not over-tall for his sixteen years, perhaps — for "eye-wit-nesses" differ in their estimates of Daniel Boone's height — or possibly taller than he looks, because his figure has the forest hunter's natural slant forward and the droop of the neck of one who must watch his path sometimes in order to tread silently. It is Squire Boone's blood which shows in his ruddy face — which would be fair but for its tan — and in the English cut of feature, the straw-colored eye-brows, and the blue eyes. But his Welsh mother's legacy is seen in the black hair that hangs long and loose in the hunter's fashion to his shoulders. We can think of Daniel Boone only as exhilarated by this plunge into the Wild. He sees ahead — the days of his great explorations and warfare, the dis-covery of Kentucky? Not at all. This is a boy of sixteen in love with his rifle. He looks ahead to vistas of forest filled with deer and to skies clouded with flocks of wild turkeys.   In that dream there is happiness enough for Daniel Boone.   Indeed, for himself, even in later life, he asked little, if any, more.   He trudges on blithely, whistling.

CHAPTER II

FOLKWAYS

THESE migrations into the inland valleys of the Old South mark the first great westward thrust of the American frontier. Thus the beginnings of the westward movement disclose to us a feature characteristic also of the later migrations which flung the frontier over the Appalachians, across the Mississippi, and finally to the shores of the Pacific. The pioneers, instead of moving westward by slow degrees, subduing the wilderness as they went, overleaped great spaces and planted themselves beyond, out of contact with the life they had left behind. Thus separated by hundreds of miles of intervening wilderness from the more civilized communities, the conquerors of the first American "West," prototypes of the conquerors of succeeding "Wests," inevitably struck out their own ways of life and developed their own customs. It would be difficult, indeed, to find anywhere a more

31

remarkable contrast in contemporary folkways than
that presented by the two great community groups
of the South — the inland or piedmont settlements,
called the Back Country, and the lowland towns
and plantations along the seaboard.

The older society of the seaboard towns, as
events were soon to prove, was not less independent in its ideals than the frontier society of the
Back Country; but it was aristocratic in tone and
feeling. Its leaders were the landed gentry — men
of elegance, and not far behind their European
contemporaries in the culture of the day. They
were rich, without effort, both from their plantations, where black slaves and indentured servants
labored, and from their coastwise and overseas
trade. Their battles with forest and red man were
long past. They had leisure for diversions such as
the chase, the breeding and racing of thoroughbred
horses, the dance, high play with dice and card, cock-
fighting, the gallantry of love, and the skill of the
rapier. Law and politics drew their soberer minds.

Very different were the conditions which confronted the pioneers in the first American "West."
There every jewel of promise was ringed round
with hostility. The cheap land the pioneer had
purchased at a nominal price, or the free land

he had taken by "tomahawk claim" — that is by cutting his name into the bark of a deadened tree, usually beside a spring — supported a forest of tall trunks and interlacing leafage. The long grass and weeds which covered the ground in a wealth of natural pasturage harbored the poisonous copperhead and the rattlesnake and, being shaded by the overhead foliage, they held the heavy dews and bred swarms of mosquitoes, gnats, and big flies which tortured both men and cattle. To protect the cattle and horses from the attacks of these pests the settlers were obliged to build large "smudges" — fires of green timber — against the wind. The animals soon learned to back up into the dense smoke and to move from one grazing spot to another as the wind changed. But useful as were the green timber fires that rolled their smoke on the wind to save the stock, they were at the same time a menace to the pioneer, for they proclaimed to roving bands of Cherokees that a further encroachment on their territory had been made by their most hated enemies — the men who felled the hunter's forest. Many an outpost pioneer who had made the long hard journey by sea and land from the old world of persecution to this new country of freedom, dropped from the

3

red man's shot ere he had hewn the threshold of his home, leaving his wife and children to the unrecorded mercy of his slayer.

Those more fortunate pioneers who settled in groups won the first heat in the battle with the wilderness through massed effort under wariness. They made their clearings in the forest, built their cabins and stockades, and planted their cornfields, while lookouts kept watch and rifles were stacked within easy reach. Every special task, such as a "raising," as cabin building was called, was undertaken by the community chiefly because the Indian danger necessitated swift building and made group action imperative. But the stanch heart is ever the glad heart. Nothing in this frontier history impresses us more than the joy of the pioneer at his labors. His determined optimism turned danger's dictation into an occasion for jollity. On the appointed day for the "raising," the neighbors would come, riding or afoot, to the newcomer's holding — the men with their rifles and axes, the women with their pots and kettles. Every child toddled along, too, helping to carry the wooden dishes and spoons. These free givers of labor had something of the Oriental's notion of the sacred ratification of friendship by a feast.

The usual dimensions of a cabin were sixteen by twenty feet. The timber for the building, having been already cut, lay at hand — logs of hickory, oak, young pine, walnut, or persimmon. To make the foundations, the men seized four of the thickest logs, laid them in place, and notched and grooved and hammered them into as close a clinch as if they had grown so. The wood must grip by its own substance alone to hold up the pioneer's dwelling, for there was not an iron nail to be had in the whole of the Back Country. Logs laid upon the foundation logs and notched into each other at the four corners formed the walls; and, when these stood at seven feet, the builders laid parallel timbers and puncheons to make both flooring and ceiling. The ridgepole of the roof was supported by two crotched trees and the roofing was made of logs and wooden slabs. The crevices of the walls were packed close with red clay and moss. Lastly, spaces for a door and windows were cut out. The door was made thick and heavy to withstand the Indian's rush. And the windowpanes? They were of paper treated with hog's fat or bear's grease.

When the sun stood overhead, the women would give the welcome call of "Dinner!" Their morning had not been less busy than the men's. They had baked corn cakes on hot stones, roasted bear or pork, or broiled venison steaks; and — above all and first of all — they had concocted the great "stew pie" without which a raising could hardly take place. This was a disputatious mixture of deer, hog, and bear — animals which, in life, would surely have companioned each other as ill! It was made in sufficient quantity to last over for supper when the day's labor was done. At supper the men took their ease on the ground, but with their rifles always in reach. If the cabin just raised by their efforts stood in the Yadkin, within sight of the great mountains the pioneers were one day to cross, perhaps a sudden bird note warning from the lookout, hidden in the brush, would bring the builders with a leap to their feet. It might be only a hunting band of friendly Catawbas that passed, or a lone Cherokee who knew that this was not his hour. If the latter, we can, in imagination, see him look once at the new house on his hunting pasture, slacken rein for a moment in front of the group of families, lift his hand in sign of peace, and silently go his way hillward. As he vanishes into the shadows, the crimson sun, sinking into the unknown wilderness beyond the mountains, pours its last glow on the roof of the cabin and on the group near its walls. With unfelt fingers, subtly, it puts the red touch of the West in the faces of the men — who have just declared, through the building of a cabin, that here is Journey's End and their abiding place.

There were community holidays among these pioneers as well as labor days, especially in the fruit season; and there were flower-picking excursions in the warm spring days. Early in April the service berry bush gleamed starrily along the watercourses, its hardy white blooms defying winter's lingering look. This bush — or tree, indeed, since it is not afraid to rear its slender trunk as high as cherry or crab apple — might well be considered emblematic of the frontier spirit in those regions where the white silence covers the earth for several months and shuts the lonely homesteader in upon himself. From the pioneer time of the Old Southwest to the last frontier of the Far North today, the service berry is cherished alike by white men and Indians; and the red men have woven about it some of their prettiest legends. When June had ripened the tree's blue-black berries, the Back Country folk went out in parties to gather them. Though the service berry was a

food staple on the frontier and its gathering a
matter of household economy, the folk made their
berry-picking jaunt a gala occasion. The women
and children with pots and baskets — the young
girls vying with each other, under the eyes of the
youths, as to who could strip boughs the fastest —
plucked gayly while the men, rifles in hand, kept
guard. For these happy summer days were also
the red man's scalping days and, at any moment,
the chatter of the picnickers might be interrupted
by the chilling war whoop. When that sound was
heard, the berry pickers raced for the fort. The
wild fruits — strawberries, service berries, cherries,
plums, crab apples — were, however, too necessary
a part of the pioneer's meager diet to be left un-
plucked out of fear of an Indian attack. Another
day would see the same group out again. The
children would keep closer to their mothers, no
doubt; and the laughter of the young girls would be
more subdued, even if their coquetry lacked nothing of its former effectiveness. Early marriages
were the rule in the Back Country and betrothals
were frequently plighted at these berry pickings.

As we consider the descriptions of the frontiersman left for us by travelers of his own day, we are
not more interested in his battles with wilderness

and Indian than in the visible effects of both wilderness and Indian upon him. His countenance
and bearing still show the European, but the European greatly altered by savage contact. The red
peril, indeed, influenced every side of frontier life.
The bands of women and children at the harvest-
ings, the log rollings, and the house raisings, were
not there merely to lighten the men's work by their
laughter and love-making. It was not safe for
them to remain in the cabins, for, to the Indian,
the cabin thus boldly thrust upon his immemorial
hunting grounds was only a secondary evil; the
greater evil was the white man's family, bespeak-
ing the increase of the dreaded palefaces. The
Indian peril trained the pioneers to alertness,
shaped them as warriors and hunters, suggested
the fashion of their dress, knit their families into
clans and the clans into a tribe wherein all were
of one spirit in the protection of each and all and a
unit of hate against their common enemy.

Too often the fields which the pioneer planted
with corn were harvested by the Indian with fire.
The hardest privations suffered by farmers and stock
were due to the settlers having to flee to the forts,
leaving to Indian devastation the crops on which
their sustenance mainly depended. Sometimes,

fortunately, the warning came in time for the frontiersman to collect his goods and chattels in his wagon and to round up his live stock and drive them safely into the common fortified enclosure. At others, the tap of the "express" — as the herald of Indian danger was called — at night on the windowpane and the low word whispered hastily, ere the "express" ran on to the next abode, meant that the Indians had surprised the outlying cabins of the settlement.

The forts were built as centrally as possible in the scattered settlements. They consisted of cabins, blockhouses, and stockades. A range of cabins often formed one side of a fort. The walls on the outside were ten or twelve feet high with roofs sloping inward. The blockhouses built at the angles of the fort projected two feet or so beyond the outer walls of the cabins and stockades, and were fitted with portholes for the watchers and the marksmen. The entrance to the fort was a large folding gate of thick slabs. It was always on the side nearest the spring. The whole structure of the fort was bullet-proof and was erected without an iron nail or spike. In the border wars these forts withstood all attacks. The savages, having proved that they could not storm them, generally laid siege and waited for thirst to compel a sortie. But the crafty besieger was as often outwitted by the equally cunning defender. Some daring soul, with silent feet and perhaps with naked body painted in Indian fashion, would drop from the wall under cover of the night, pass among the foemen to the spring, and return to the fort with water.

Into the pioneer's phrase-making the Indian influence penetrated so that he named seasons for his foe. So thoroughly has the term "Indian Summer," now to us redolent of charm, become disassociated from its origins that it gives us a shock to be reminded that to these Back Country folk the balmy days following on the cold snap meant the season when the red men would come back for a last murderous raid on the settlements before winter should seal up the land. The "Powwowing Days" were the mellow days in the latter part of February, when the red men in council made their medicine and learned of their redder gods whether or no they should take the warpath when the sap pulsed the trees into leaf. Even the children at their play acknowledged the red-skinned schoolmaster, for their chief games were a training in his woodcraft and in the use of his weapons. Tomahawk-throwing was a favorite sport because of its gruesome practical purposes. The boys must learn to gauge the tomahawk's revolutions by the distance of the throw so as to bury the blade in its objective. Swift running and high jumping through the brush and fallen timber were sports that taught agility in escape. The boys learned to shoot accurately the long rifles of their time, with a log or a forked stick for a rest, and a moss pad under the barrel to keep it from jerking and spoiling the aim. They wrestled with each other, mastered the tricks of throwing an opponent, and learned the scalp hold instead of the toe hold. It was part of their education to imitate the noises of every bird and beast of the forest. So they learned to lure the turkey within range, or by the bleat of a fawn to bring her dam to the rifle. A well-simulated wolf's howl would call forth a response and so inform the lone hunter of the vicinity of the pack. This forest speech was not only the language of diplomacy in the hunting season; it was the borderer's secret code in war. Stray Indians put themselves in touch again with the band by turkey calls in the daytime and by owl or wolf notes at night. The frontiersmen used the same means to trick the Indian band into betraying the place of its ambuscade, or to lure the strays, unwitting, within reach of the knife.

In that age, before the forests had given place to farms and cities and when the sun had but slight acquaintance with the sod, the summers were cool and the winters long and cold in the Back Country. Sometimes in September severe frosts destroyed the corn. The first light powdering called "hunting snows" fell in October, and then the men of the Back Country set out on the chase. Their object was meat — buffalo, deer, elk, bear — for the winter larder, and skins to send out in the spring by pack-horses to the coast in trade for iron, steel, and salt. The rainfall in North Carolina was much heavier than in Virginia and, from autumn into early winter, the Yadkin forests were sheeted with rain; but wet weather, so far from deterring the hunter, aided him to the kill. In blowing rain, he knew he would find the deer herding in the sheltered places on the hillsides. In windless rain, he knew that his quarry ranged the open woods and the high places. The fair play of the pioneer held it a great disgrace to kill a deer in winter when the heavy frost had crusted the deep snow. On the crust men and wolves could travel with ease, but the deer's sharp hoofs pierced through and made him defenseless. Wolves and dogs destroyed great quantities of deer caught in this way; and men who shot deer under these conditions were considered no huntsmen. There was, indeed, a practical side to this chivalry of the chase, for meat and pelt were both poor at this season; but the true hunter also obeyed the finer tenet of his code, for he would go to the rescue of deer caught in the crusts — and he killed many a wolf sliding over the ice to an easy meal.

The community moral code of the frontier was brief and rigorous. What it lacked of the "whereas" and "inasmuch" of legal ink it made up in sound hickory. In fact, when we review the activities of this solid yet elastic wood in the moral, social, and economic phases of Back Country life, we are moved to wonder if the pioneers would have been the same race of men had they been nurtured beneath a less strenuous and adaptable vegetation! The hickory gave the frontiersman wood for all implements and furnishings where the demand was equally for lightness, strength, and elasticity. It provided his straight logs for building, his block mortars — hollowed by fire and stone — for corn-grinding, his solid plain furniture, his axles, rifle butts, ax handles, and so forth. It supplied

his magic wand for the searching out of iniquity
in the junior members of his household, and his
most cogent argument, as a citizen, in convincing
the slothful, the blasphemous, or the dishonest
adult whose errors disturbed communal harmony.
Its nuts fed his hogs. Before he raised stock, the
unripe hickory nuts, crushed for their white liquid,
supplied him with butter for his corn bread and
helped out his store of bear's fat. Both the name
and the knowledge of the uses of this tree came
to the earliest pioneers through contact with the
red man, whose hunting bow and fishing spear and
the hobbles for his horses were fashioned of the
"pohickory" tree. The Indian women first made
pohickory butter, and the wise old men of the
Cherokee towns, so we are told, first applied the
pohickory rod to the vanity of youth!

A glance at the interior of a log cabin in the
Back Country of Virginia or North Carolina would
show, in primitive design, what is, perhaps, after
all the perfect home — a place where the personal
life and the work life are united and where nothing
futile finds space. Every object in the cabin was
practical and had been made by hand on the spot
to answer a need. Besides the chairs hewn from
hickory blocks, there were others made of slabs

set on three legs. A large slab or two with four legs served as a movable table; the permanent table was built against the wall, its outer edge held up by two sticks. The low bed was built into the wall in the same way and softened for slumber by a mattress of pine needles, chaff, or dried moss. In the best light from the greased paper windowpanes stood the spinning wheel and loom, on which the housewife made cloth for the family's garments. Over the fireplace or beside the doorway, and suspended usually on stags' antlers, hung the firearms and the yellow powderhorns, the latter often carved in Indian fashion with scenes of the hunt or war. On a shelf or on pegs were the wooden spoons, plates, bowls, and noggins. Also near the fireplace, which was made of large flat stones with a mud-plastered log chimney, stood the grinding block for making hominy. If it were an evening in early spring, the men of the household would be tanning and dressing deerskins to be sent out with the trade caravan, while the women sewed, made moccasins or mended them, in the light of pine knots or candles of bear's grease. The larger children might be weaving cradles for the babies, Indian fashion, out of hickory twigs; and there would surely be a sound of whetting steel, for scalping knives and tomahawks must be kept keen-tempered now that the days have come when the red gods whisper their chant of war through the young leafage.

The Back Country folk, as they came from several countries, generally settled in national groups, each preserving its own speech and its own religion, each approaching frontier life through its own native temperament. And the frontier met each and all alike, with the same need and the same menace, and molded them after one general pattern. If the cabin stood in a typical Virginian settlement where the folk were of English stock, it may be that the dulcimer and some old love song of the homeland enlivened the work — or perhaps chairs were pushed back and young people danced the country dances of the homeland and the Virginia Reel, for these Virginian English were merry folk, and their religion did not frown upon the dance. In a cabin on the Shenandoah or the upper Yadkin the German tongue clicked away over the evening dish of kraut or sounded more sedately in a Lutheran hymn; while from some herder's hut on the lower Yadkin the wild note of the bagpipes or of the ancient four-stringed harp mingled with the Gaelic speech.

Among the homes in the Shenandoah where old England's ways prevailed, none was gayer than the tavern kept by the man whom the good Moravian Brother called "Severe." There perhaps the feasting celebrated the nuptials of John Sevier, who was barely past his seventeenth birthday when he took to himself a wife. Or perhaps the dancing, in moccasined feet on the puncheon flooring, was a ceremonial to usher into Back Country life the new municipality John had just organized, for John at nineteen had taken his earliest step towards his larger career, which we shall follow later on, as the architect of the first little governments beyond the mountains.

In the Boone home on the Yadkin, we may guess that the talk was solely of the hunt, unless young Daniel had already become possessed of his first compass and was studying its ways. On such an evening, while the red afterglow lingered, he might be mending a passing trader's firearms by the fires of the primitive forge his father had set up near the trading path running from Hillsborough to the Catawba towns. It was said by the local nimrods that none could doctor a sick rifle better than young Daniel Boone, already the master huntsman of them all. And perhaps some trader's tale, told when the caravan halted for the night, kindled the youth's first desire to penetrate the mountain-guarded wilderness, for the tales of these Roma-nies of commerce were as the very badge of their free-masonry, and entry money at the doors of strangers.

Out on the border's edge, heedless of the shadow of the mountains looming between the newly built cabin and that western land where they and their kind were to write the fame of the Ulster Scot in a shining script that time cannot dull, there might sit a group of stern-faced men, all deep in discussion of some point of spiritual doctrine or of the tem-poral rights of men. Yet, in every cabin, what-ever the national differences, the setting was the same The spirit of the frontier was modeling out of old clay a new Adam to answer the needs of a new earth.

It would be far less than just to leave the Back Country folk without further reference to the de-voted labors of their clergy. In the earliest days the settlers were cut off from their church systems; the pious had to maintain their piety unaided, ex-cept in the rare cases where a pastor accompanied a group of settlers of his denomination into the wilds. One of the first ministers who fared into

4

the Back Country to remind the Ulster Presbyterians of their spiritual duties was the Reverend
Hugh McAden of Philadelphia. He made long
itineraries under the greatest hardships, in constant danger from Indians and wild beasts, carrying the counsel of godliness to the far scattered
flock. Among the Highland settlements the Reverend James Campbell for thirty years traveled
about, preaching each Sunday at some gathering
point a sermon in both English and Gaelic. A
little later, in the Yadkin Valley, after Craighead's
day there arose a small school of Presbyterian
ministers whose zeal and fearlessness in the
cause of religion and of just government had an
influence on the frontiersmen that can hardly be
overestimated.

But, in the beginning, the pioneer encountered
the savagery of border life, grappled with it, and
reacted to it without guidance from other men-
tor than his own instincts. His need was still the
primal threefold need — family, sustenance, and
safe sleep when the day's work was done. We who
look back with thoughtful eyes upon the frontiersman — all links of contact with his racial past
severed, at grips with destruction in the contenting
of his needs — see something more, something

larger, than he saw in the log cabin raised by his hands, its structure held together solely by his close grooving and fitting of its own strength. Though the walls he built for himself have gone with his own dust back to the earth, the symbol he erected for us stands.

CHAPTER III

THE trader was the first pathfinder. His caravans began the change of purpose that was to come to the Indian warrior's route, turning it slowly into the beaten track of communication and commerce. The settlers, the rangers, the surveyors, went westward over the trails which he had blazed for them years before. Their enduring works are commemorated in the cities and farms which today lie along every ancient border line; but of their forerunner's hazardous Indian trade nothing remains. Let us therefore pay a moment's homage here to the trader, who first — to borrow a phrase from Indian speech — made white for peace the red trails of war.

He was the first cattleman of the Old Southwest. Fifty years before John Findlay,[1] one of this class of pioneers, led Daniel Boone through Cumberland

[1] The name is spelled in various ways: Findlay, Finlay, Findley

52

Gap, the trader's bands of horses roamed the western slopes of the Appalachian Mountains and his cattle grazed among the deer on the green banks of the old Cherokee (Tennessee) River. He was the pioneer settler beyond the high hills; for he built, in the center of the Indian towns, the first white man's cabin — with its larger annex, the trading house — and dwelt there during the greater part of the year. He was America's first magnate of international commerce. His furs — for which he paid in guns, knives, ammunition, vermilion paint, mirrors, and cloth — lined kings' mantles, and hatted the Lords of Trade as they strode to their council chamber in London to discuss his business and to pass those regulations which might have seriously hampered him but for his resourcefulness in circumventing them!

He was the first frontier warrior, for he either fought off or fell before small parties of hostile Indians who, in the interest of the Spanish or French, raided his pack-horse caravans on the march. Often, too, side by side with the red brothers of his adoption, he fought in the intertribal wars. His was the first educative and civilizing influence in the Indian towns. He endeavored to cure the Indians of their favorite midsummer madness, war, by inducing them to raise stock and poultry and improve their corn, squash, and pea gardens. It is not necessary to impute to him philanthropic motives. He was a practical man and he saw that war hurt his trade: it endangered his summer caravans and hampered the autumn hunt for deerskins.

In the earliest days of the eighteenth century, when the colonists of Virginia and the Carolinas were only a handful, it was the trader who defeated each successive attempt of French and Spanish agents to weld the tribes into a confederacy for the annihilation of the English settlements. The English trader did his share to prevent what is now the United States from becoming a part of a Latin empire and to save it for a race having the Anglo-Saxon ideal and speaking the English tongue.

The colonial records of the period contain items which, taken singly, make small impression on the casual reader but which, listed together, throw a strong light on the past and bring that mercenary figure, the trader, into so bold a relief that the design verges on the heroic. If we wonder, for instance, why the Scotch Highlanders who settled in the wilds at the headwaters of the Cape Fear River, about 1729, and were later followed by Welsh and Huguenots, met with no opposition from the Indians, the mystery is solved when we discover, almost by accident, a few printed lines which record that, in 1700, the hostile natives on the Cape Fear were subdued to the English and brought into friendly alliance with them by Colonel William Bull, a trader. We read further and learn that the Spaniards in Florida had long endeavored to unite the tribes in Spanish and French territory against the English and that the influence of traders prevented the consummation. The Spaniards, in 1702, had prepared to invade English territory with nine hundred Indians. The plot was discovered by Creek Indians and disclosed to their friends, the traders, who immediately gathered together five hundred warriors, marched swiftly to meet the invaders, and utterly routed them. Again, when the Indians, incited by the Spanish at St. Augustine, rose against the English in 1715, and the Yamasi Massacre occurred in South Carolina, it was due to the traders that some of the settlements at least were not wholly unprepared to defend themselves.

The early English trader was generally an intelligent man; sometimes educated, nearly always fearless and resourceful. He knew the one sure basis on which men of alien blood and far separated stages of moral and intellectual development can meet in understanding — namely, the truth of the spoken word. He recognized honor as the bond of trade and the warp and woof of human intercourse. The uncorrupted savage also had his plain interpretation of the true word in the mouths of men, and a name for it. He called it the "Old Beloved Speech"; and he gave his confidence to the man who spoke this speech even in the close barter for furs.

We shall find it worth while to refer to the map of America as it was in the early days of the colonial fur trade, about the beginning of the eighteenth century. A narrow strip of loosely strung English settlements stretched from the north border of New England to the Florida line. North Florida was Spanish territory. On the far distant southwestern borders of the English colonies were the southern possessions of France. The French sphere of influence extended up the Mississippi, and thence by way of rivers and the Great Lakes to its base in Canada on the borders of New England and New York. In South Carolina dwelt the Yamasi tribe of about three thousand warriors, their chief towns only sixty or eighty miles distant from the Spanish town of St. Augustine. On the

west, about the same distance northeast of New
Orleans, in what is now Alabama and Georgia, lay
the Creek nation. There French garrisons held Mobile and Fort Alabama. The Creeks at this time
numbered over four thousand warriors. The lands
of the Choctaws, a tribe of even larger fighting
strength, began two hundred miles north of New
Orleans and extended along the Mississippi. A
hundred and sixty miles northeast of the Choctaw towns were the Chickasaws, the bravest and
most successful warriors of all the tribes south of
the Iroquois. The Cherokees, in part seated within
the Carolinas, on the upper courses of the Savannah
River, mustered over six thousand men at arms.
East of them were the Catawba towns. North of
them were the Shawanoes and Delawares, in easy
communication with the tribes of Canada. Still
farther north, along the Mohawk and other rivers
joining with the Hudson and Lake Ontario stood
the "long houses" of the fiercest and most warlike of all the savages, the Iroquois or Six Nations.

The Indians along the English borders out-
numbered the colonists perhaps ten to one. If the
Spanish and the French had succeeded in the conspiracy to unite on their side all the tribes, a red
billow of tomahawk wielders would have engulfed

and extinguished the English settlements. The
French, it is true, made allies of the Shawanoes,
the Delawares, the Choctaws, and a strong faction of the Creeks; and they finally won over
the Cherokees after courting them for more than
twenty years. But the Creeks in part, the powerful Chickasaws, and the Iroquois Confederacy,
or Six Nations, remained loyal to the English. In
both North and South it was the influence of the
traders that kept these red tribes on the English side. The Iroquois were held loyal by Sir
William Johnson and his deputy, George Croghan,
the "King of Traders." The Chickasaws followed their "best-beloved" trader, James Adair;
and among the Creeks another trader, Lachlan
McGillivray, wielded a potent influence.

Lachlan McGillivray was a Highlander. He
landed in Charleston in 1735 at the age of sixteen
and presently joined a trader's caravan as pack-
horse boy. A few years later he married a woman
of the Creeks. On many occasions he defeated
French and Spanish plots with the Creeks for
the extermination of the colonists in Georgia and
South Carolina. His action in the final war with
the French (1760), when the Indian terror was
raging, is typical. News came that four thousand

Creek warriors, reinforced by French Choctaws, were about to fall on the southern settlements. At the risk of their lives, McGillivray and another trader named Galphin hurried from Charleston to their trading house on the Georgia frontier. Thither they invited several hundred Creek warriors, feasted and housed them for several days, and finally won them from their purpose. McGillivray had a brilliant son, Alexander, who about this time became a chief in his mother's nation — perhaps on this very occasion, as it was an Indian custom, in making a brotherhood pact, to send a son to dwell in the brother's house. We shall meet that son again as the Chief of the Creeks and the terrible scourge of Georgia and Tennessee in the dark days of the Revolutionary War.

The bold deeds of the early traders, if all were to be told, would require a book as long as the huge volume written by James Adair, the "English Chickasaw." Adair was an Englishman who entered the Indian trade in 1735 and launched upon the long and dangerous trail from Charleston to the upper towns of the Cherokees, situated in the present Monroe County, Tennessee. Thus he was one of the earliest pioneers of the Old Southwest; and he was Tennessee's first author. "I am well acquainted," he says, "with near two thousand miles of the American continent" — a statement which gives one some idea of an early trader's enterprise, hardihood, and peril. Adair's "two thousand miles" were twisting Indian trails and paths he slashed out for himself through uninhabited wilds, for when not engaged in trade, hunting, literature, or war, it pleased him to make solitary trips of exploration. These seem to have led him chiefly northward through the Appalachians, of which he must have been one of the first white explorers.

A many-sided man was James Adair — cultured, for his style suffers not by comparison with other writers of his day, no stranger to Latin and Greek, and not ignorant of Hebrew, which he studied to assist him in setting forth his ethnological theory that the American Indians were the descendants of the Ten Lost Tribes of Israel. Before we dismiss his theory with a smile, let us remember that he had not at his disposal the data now available which reveal points of likeness in custom, language formation, and symbolism among almost all primitive peoples. The formidable title-page of his book in itself suggests an author keenly observant, accurate as to detail, and possessed of a versatile and substantial mind. Most of the pages were written in the towns of the Chickasaws, with whom he lived "as a friend and brother," but from whose "natural jealousy" and "prying disposition" he was obliged to conceal his papers. "Never," he assures us, "was a literary work begun and carried on with more disadvantages!"

Despite these disabilities the author wrote a book of absorbing interest. His intimate sympathetic pictures of Indian life as it was before the tribes had been conquered are richly valuable to the lover of native lore and to the student of the history of white settlement. The author believes, as he must, in the supremacy of his own race, but he nevertheless presents the Indians' side of the argument as no man could who had not made himself one of them. He thereby adds interest to those fierce struggles which took place along the border; for he shows us the red warrior not as a mere brute with a tomahawk but as a human creature with an ideal of his own, albeit an ideal that must give place to a better. Even in view of the red man's hideous methods of battle and inhuman treatment of captives, we cannot ponder unmoved Adair's description of his preparations for war — the fasting, the abstention from all family

intercourse, and the purification rites and prayers
for three days in the house set apart, while the
women, who might not come close to their men in
this fateful hour, stood throughout the night till
dawn chanting before the door. Another poetic
touch the author gives us, from the Cherokee — or
Cheerake as he spells it — explaining that the root,
chee-ra, means fire. A Cherokee never extinguished
fire save on the occasion of a death, when he thrust
a burning torch into the water and said, *Neetah in-
tahah* — "the days appointed him were finished."
The warrior slain in battle was held to have been
balanced by death and it was said of him that "he
was weighed on the path and made light." Adair
writes that the Cherokees, until corrupted by French
agents and by the later class of traders who poured
rum among them like water, were honest, industri-
ous, and friendly. They were ready to meet the
white man with their customary phrase of good will:
"I shall firmly shake hands with your speech."
He was intimately associated with this tribe from
1735 to 1744, when he diverted his activities to
the Chickasaws.

It was from the Cherokees' chief town, Great
Telliko, in the Appalachians, that Adair explored
the mountains. He describes the pass through the

chain which was used by the Indians and which, from his outline of it, was probably the Cumberland Gap. He relates many incidents of the struggle with the French — manifestations even in this remote wilderness of the vast conflict that was being waged for the New World by two imperial nations of the Old.

Adair undertook, at the solicitation of Governor Glen of South Carolina, the dangerous task of opening up trade with the Choctaws, a tribe mustering upwards of five thousand warriors who were wholly in the French interest. Their country lay in what is now the State of Mississippi along the great river, some seven hundred miles west and southwest of Charleston. After passing the friendly Creek towns the trail led on for 150 miles through what was practically the enemy's country. Adair, owing to what he likes to term his "usual good fortune," reached the Choctaw country safely and by his adroitness and substantial presents won the friendship of the influential chief, Red Shoe, whom he found in a receptive mood, owing to a French agent's breach of hospitality involving Red Shoe's favorite wife. Adair thus created a large pro-English faction among the Choctaws, and his success seriously impaired French prestige with all the southwestern tribes. Several times French Choctaws bribed to murder him, waylaid Adair on the trail — twice when he was alone — only to be baffled by the imperturbable self-possession and alert wit which never failed him in emergencies.

Winning a Choctaw trade cost Adair, besides attacks on his life, £2200, for which he was never reimbursed, notwithstanding Governor Glen's agreement with him. And, on his return to Charleston, while the Governor was detaining him "on one pretext or another," he found that a new expedition, which the Governor was favoring for reasons of his own, had set out to capture his Chickasaw trade and gather in "the expected great crop of deerskins and beaver . . . before I could possibly return to the Chikkasah Country." Nothing daunted, however, the hardy trader set out alone.

In the severity of winter, frost, snow, hail and heavy rains succeed each other in these climes, so that I partly rode and partly swam to the Chikkasah country; for not expecting to stay long below [in Charleston] I took no leathern canoe. Many of the broad, deep creeks . . . had now overflowed their banks, ran at a rapid rate and were unpassable to any but *desperate people*: . . . the rivers and swamps were dreadful by rafts of timber driving down the former and the great fallen trees floating in the latter. . . . Being forced to wade deep through cane swamps or woody thickets, it proved very

troublesome to keep my firearms dry on which, as a
second means, my life depended.

Nevertheless Adair defeated the Governor's attempt to steal his trade, and later on published
the whole story in the Charleston press and sent
in a statement of his claims to the Assembly,
with frank observations on His Excellency himself. We gather that his bold disregard of High
Personages set all Charleston in an uproar!

Adair is tantalizingly modest about his own
deeds. He devotes pages to prove that an Indian
rite agrees with the Book of Leviticus but only a
paragraph to an exploit of courage and endurance
such as that ride and swim for the Indian trade.
We have to read between the lines to find the man;
but he well repays the search. Briefly, incidentally,
he mentions that on one trip he was captured by
the French, who were so

well acquainted with the great damages I had done to
them and feared others I might occasion, as to confine
me a close prisoner . . . in the Alebahma garrison. They
were fully resolved to have sent me down to Mobile or
New Orleans as a capital criminal to be hanged . . .
*but I doubted not of being able to extricate myself some way
or other*. They appointed double centries over me for
some days before I was to be sent down in the French
King's large boat. They were strongly charged against

5

laying down their weapons or suffering any hostile thing to be in the place where I was kept, as they deemed me capable of any mischief. . . . About an hour before we were to set off by water I escaped from them by land. . . . I took through the middle of the low land covered with briers at full speed. I heard the French clattering on horseback along the path . . . and the howling savages pursuing . . . , but *my usual good fortune* enabled me to leave them far enough behind. . . .

One feels that a few of the pages given up to Leviticus might well have been devoted to a detailed account of this escape from "double centries" and a fortified garrison, and the plunge through the tangled wilds, by a man without gun or knife or supplies, and who for days dared not show himself upon the trail.

There is too much of "my usual good fortune" in Adair's narrative; such luck as his argues for extraordinary resources in the man. Sometimes we discover only through one phrase on a page that he must himself have been the hero of an event he relates in the third person. This seems to be the case in the affair of Priber, which was the worst of those "damages" Adair did to the French. Priber was "a gentleman of curious and speculative temper" sent by the French in 1736 to Great Telliko to win the Cherokees to their interest.

At this time Adair was trading with the Cherokees. He relates that Priber,

more effectually to answer the design of his commission
. . . ate, drank, slept, danced, dressed, and painted himself with the Indians, so that it was not easy to distinguish him from the natives, — he married also with them, and being endued with a strong understanding and retentive memory he soon learned their dialect, and by gradual advances impressed them with a very ill opinion of the English, representing them as fraudulent, avaritious and encroaching people; he at the same time inflated the artless savages with a prodigious high opinion of their own importance in the American scale of power. . . . Having thus infected them . . . he easily formed them into a nominal republican government — crowned their old Archi-magus emperor after a pleasing new savage form, and invented a variety of high-sounding titles for all the members of his imperial majesty's red court.

Priber cemented the Cherokee empire "by slow but sure degrees to the very great danger of our southern colonies." His position was that of Secretary of State and as such, with a studiedly provocative arrogance, he carried on correspondence with the British authorities. The colonial Government seems, on this occasion, to have listened to the traders and to have realized that Priber was a danger, for soldiers were sent to take him prisoner. The Cherokees, however, had so firmly "shaked hands" with their Secretary's admired discourse that they threatened to take the warpath if their beloved man were annoyed, and the soldiers went home without him — to the great hurt of English prestige. The Cherokee empire had now endured for five years and was about to rise "into a far greater state of puissance by the acquisition of the Muskohge, Chocktaw and the Western Mississippi Indians," when fortunately for the history of British colonization in America, "an accident befell the Secretary."

It is in connection with this "accident" that the reader suspects the modest but resourceful Adair of conniving with Fate. Since the military had failed and the Government dared not again employ force, other means must be found; the trader provided them. The Secretary with his Cherokee bodyguard journeyed south on his mission to the Creeks. Secure, as he supposed, he lodged overnight in an Indian town. But there a company of English traders took him into custody, along with his bundle of manuscripts presumably intended for the French commandant at Fort Alabama, and handed him over to the Governor of Georgia, who imprisoned him and kept him out of mischief till he died.

As a Briton, Adair contributed to Priber's fate;

and as such he approves it. As a scholar with philosophical and ethnological leanings, however, he deplores it, and hopes that Priber's valuable manuscripts may "escape the despoiling hands of military power." Priber had spent his leisure in compiling a Cherokee dictionary; Adair's occupation, while domiciled in his winter house in Great Telliko, was the writing of his Indian Appendix to the Pentateuch. As became brothers in science, they had exchanged notes, so we gather from Adair's references to conversations and correspondence. Adair's difficulties as an author, however, had been increased by a treacherous lapse from professional etiquette on the part of the Secretary: "He told them [the Indians] that in the very same manner as he was their great Secretary, I was the devil's clerk, or an accursed one who marked on paper the bad speech of the evil ones of darkness." On his own part Adair admits that his object in this correspondence was to trap the Secretary into something more serious than literary errata. That is, he admits it by implication; he says the Secretary "feared" it. During the years of their duel, Adair apparently knew that the scholarly compiler of the Cherokee dictionary was secretly inciting members of this particular Lost Tribe to tomahawk the discoverer of

their biblical origin; and Priber, it would seem,
knew that he knew!

Adair shows, inferentially, that land encroachment was not the sole cause of those Indian wars
with which we shall deal in a later chapter. The
earliest causes were the instigations of the French
and the rewards which they offered for English
scalps. But equally provocative of Indian ran-
cor were the acts of sometimes merely stupid,
sometimes dishonest, officials; the worst of these,
Adair considered, was the cheapening of the trade
through the granting of general licenses.

Formerly each trader had a license for two [Indian] towns.
. . . At my first setting out among them, a number of
traders . . . journeyed through our various nations in
different companies and were generally men of worth; of
course they would have a living price for their goods,
which they carried on horseback to the remote Indian
countries at very great expences. . . . [The Indians]
were kept under proper restraint, were easy in their
minds and peaceable on account of the plain, honest
lessons daily inculcated on them . . . but according to
the present unwise plan, two and even three Arablike
peddlars sculk about in one of those villages . . . who
are generally the dregs and off-scourings of our climes
. . . by inebriating the Indians with their nominally
prohibited and poisoning spirits, they purchase the
necessaries of life at four and five hundred per cent

cheaper than the orderly traders. . . . Instead of showing good examples of moral conduct, beside the other part of life, they instruct the unknowing and imitating savages in many diabolical lessons of obscenity and blasphemy.

In these statements, contemporary records bear him out. There is no sadder reading than the many pleas addressed by the Indian chiefs to various officials to stop the importation of liquor into their country, alleging the debauchment of their young men and warning the white man, with whom they desired to be friends, that in an Indian drink and blood lust quickly combined.

Adair's book was published in London in 1775. He wrote it to be read by Englishmen as well as Americans; and some of his reflections on liberty, justice, and Anglo-Saxon unity would not sound unworthily today. His sympathies were with "the principles of our Magna Charta Americana"; but he thought the threatened division of the English-speaking peoples the greatest evil that could befall civilization. His voluminous work discloses a man not only of wide mental outlook but a practical man with a sense of commercial values. Yet, instead of making a career for himself among his own caste, he made his home for over thirty years in the Chickasaw towns; and it is plain that, with the exception of some of his older brother traders, he preferred the Chickasaw to any other society.

The complete explanation of such men as Adair we need not expect to find stated anywhere — not even in and between the lines of his book. The conventionalist would seek it in moral obliquity; the radical, in a temperament that is irked by the superficialities that comprise so large a part of conventional standards. The reason for his being what he was is almost the only thing Adair did not analyze in his book. Perhaps, to him, it was self-evident. We may let it be so to us, and see it most clearly presented in a picture composed from some of his brief sketches: A land of grass and green shade inset with bright waters, where deer and domestic cattle herded together along the banks; a circling group of houses, their white-clayed walls sparkling under the sun's rays, and, within and without, the movement of "a friendly and sagacious people," who "kindly treated and watchfully guarded" their white brother in peace and war, and who conversed daily with him in the Old Beloved Speech learned first of Nature. "Like towers in cities beyond the common size of those of the Indians" rose the winter and summer houses

and the huge trading house which the tribe had
built for their best beloved friend in the town's
center, because there he would be safest from attack. On the rafters hung the smoked and bar-
becued delicacies taken in the hunt and prepared
for him by his red servants, who were also his comrades at home and on the dangerous trail. "Beloved old women" kept an eye on his small sons,
put to drowse on panther skins so that they might
grow up brave warriors. Nothing was there of
artifice or pretense, only "the needful things to
make a reasonable life happy." All was as primitive, naïve, and contented as the woman whose
outline is given once in a few strokes, proudly and
gayly penciled: "I have the pleasure of writing
this by the side of a Chikkasah female, as great a
princess as ever lived among the ancient Peruvians
or Mexicans, and she bids me be sure not to mark
the paper wrong after the manner of most of the
traders; otherwise it will spoil the making good
bread or homony!"

His final chapter is the last news of James Adair,
type of the earliest trader. Did his bold attacks
on corrupt officials and rum peddlers — made publicly before Assemblies and in print — raise for
him a dense cloud of enmity that dropped oblivion

on his memory? Perhaps. But, in truth, his own book is all the history of him we need. It is the record of a man. He lived a full life and served his day; and it matters not that a mist envelops the place where unafraid he met the Last Enemy, was "weighed on the path and made light."

CHAPTER IV

THE great pile of the Appalachian peaks was not the only barrier which held back the settler with his plough and his rifle from following the trader's tinkling caravans into the valleys beyond. Over the hills the French were lords of the land. The frontiersman had already felt their enmity through the torch and tomahawk of their savage allies. By his own strength alone he could not cope with the power entrenched beyond the hills; so he halted. But that power, by its unachievable desire to be overlord of two hemispheres, was itself to precipitate events which would open the westward road.

The recurring hour in the cycle of history, when the issue of Autocracy against Democracy cleaves the world, struck for the men of the eighteenth century as the second half of that century dawned. In our own day, happily, that issue has been perceived by the rank and file of the people. In those darker days, as France and England grappled in that conflict of systems which culminated in the Seven Years' War, the fundamental principles at stake were clear to only a handful of thinking men.

But abstractions, whether clear or obscure, do not cause ambassadors to demand their passports. The declaration of war awaits the overt act. Behold, then, how great a matter is kindled by a little fire! The *casus belli* between France and England in the Seven Years' War — the war which humbled France in Europe and lost her India and Canada — had to do with a small log fort built by a few Virginians in 1754 at the Forks of the Ohio River and wrested from them in the same year by a company of Frenchmen from Canada.

The French claimed the valley of the Ohio as their territory; the English claimed it as theirs. The dispute was of long standing. The French claim was based on discovery; the English claim, on the sea-to-sea charters of Virginia and other colonies and on treaties with the Six Nations. The French refused to admit the right of the Six Nations to dispose of the territory. The English were inclined to maintain the validity of their treaties with the Indians. Especially was Virginia so inclined, for a large share of the Ohio lay within her chartered domain.

The quarrel had entered its acute phase in 1749, when both the rival claimants took action to assert their sovereignty. The Governor of Canada sent an envoy, Céloron de Blainville, with soldiers, to take formal possession of the Ohio for the King of France. In the same year the English organized in Virginia the Ohio Company for the colonization of the same country; and summoned Christopher Gist, explorer, trader, and guide, from his home on the Yadkin and dispatched him to survey the land.

Then appeared on the scene that extraordinary man, Robert Dinwiddie, Lieutenant Governor of Virginia, erstwhile citizen of Glasgow. His correspondence from Virginia during his seven years' tenure of office (1751–58) depicts the man with a vividness surpassing paint. He was as honest as the day — as honest as he was fearless and fussy. But he had no patience; he wanted things done and done at once, and his way was *the* way to do them. People who did not think as he thought didn't *think* at all. On this drastic premise he went to work. There was of course continuous friction between him and the House of Burgesses.

Dinwiddie had all a Scot's native talent for sarcasm. His letters, his addresses, perhaps in particular his addresses to the House, bristled with satirical thrusts at his opponents. If he had spelled out in full all the words he was so eager to write, he would have been obliged to lessen his output; so he used a shorthand system of his own, peculiar enough to be remarkable even though abbreviations were the rule in that day. Even the dignity of Kings he sacrificed to speed, and we find "His Majesty" abbreviated to "H M'y"; yet a smaller luminary known as "His Honor" fares better, losing only the last letter — "His Hono." "Ho." stands for "house" and "yt" for "that," "what," "it," and "anything else," as convenient. Many of his letters wind up with "I am ve'y much fatig'd." We know that he must have been!

It was a formidable task that confronted Dinwiddie — to possess and defend the Ohio. Christopher Gist returned in 1751, having surveyed the valley for the Ohio Company as far as the Scioto and Miami rivers, and in the following year the survey was ratified by the Indians. The Company's men were busy blazing trails through the territory and building fortified posts. But the French dominated the territory. They had built and occupied with troops Fort Le Bœuf on French Creek, a stream flowing into the Allegheny. We may imagine Dinwiddie's rage at this violation of British soil by French soldiers and how he must have sputtered to the young George Washington, when he summoned that officer and made him the bearer of a letter to the French commander at Fort Le Bœuf, to demand that French troops be at once withdrawn from the Ohio.

Washington made the journey to Fort Le Bœuf in December, 1753, but the mission of course proved fruitless. Dinwiddie then wrote to London urging that a force be sent over to help the colonies maintain their rights and, under orders from the Crown, suggested by himself, he wrote to the governors of all the other colonies to join with Virginia in raising troops to settle the ownership of the disputed territory. From Governor Dobbs of North Carolina he received an immediate response. By means of logic, sarcasm, and the entire force of his prerogatives, Dinwiddie secured from his own balking Assembly £10,000 with which to raise troops. From Maryland he obtained nothing. There were three prominent Marylanders in the Ohio Company, but — or because of this — the Maryland Assembly voted down the measure for a military appropriation. On June 18, 1754, Dinwiddie wrote, with unusually full spelling for him:

I am perswaded had His Majesty's Com'ds to the other Colonies been duely obey'd, and the necessary Assistance given by them, the Fr. wou'd have long ago have been oblig'd entirely to have evacuated their usurp'd Possession of the King's Lands, instead of w'ch they are daily becoming more formidable, whilst every Gov't except No. Caro. has amus'd me with Expectations that have proved fruitless, and at length refuse to give any Supply, unless in such a manner as must render it ineffectual.

This saddened mood with its deliberate penmanship did not last long. Presently Dinwiddie was making a Round Robin of himself in another series of letters to Governors, Councilors, and Assemblymen, frantically beseeching them for "H. M'y's hono." and their own, and, if not, for "post'r'ty," to rise against the cruel French whose Indians were harrying the borders again and "Basely, like Virmin, stealing and carrying off the helpless infant" — as nice a simile, by the way, as any Sheridan ever put into the mouth of Mrs. Malaprop.

Dinwiddie saw his desires thwarted on every hand by the selfish spirit of localism and jealousy which was more rife in America in those days than it is today. Though the phrase "capitalistic war" had not yet been coined, the great issues of English civilization on this continent were befogged, for the majority in the colonies, by the trivial fact that the shareholders in the Ohio Company stood to win by a vigorous prosecution of the war and to lose if it were not prosecuted at all. The irascible Governor, however, proceeded with such men and means as he could obtain.

And now in the summer of 1754 came the "overt act" which precipitated the inevitable war. The key to the valley of the Ohio was the tongue of land at the Forks, where the Allegheny and the Monongahela join their waters in the Beautiful River. This site — today Pittsburgh — if occupied and held by either nation would give that nation the command of the Ohio. Occupied it was for a brief hour by a small party of Virginians, under Captain William Trent; but no sooner had they erected on the spot a crude fort than the French descended upon them. What happened then all the world knows: how the French built on the captured site their great Fort Duquesne; how George Washington with an armed force, sent by Dinwiddie to recapture the place, encountered French and Indians at Great Meadows and built Fort Necessity, which he was compelled to surrender;

6

how in the next year (1755) General Braddock arrived from across the sea and set out to take Fort Duquesne, only to meet on the way the disaster called "Braddock's Defeat"; and how, before another year had passed, the Seven Years' War was raging in Europe, and England was allied with the enemies of France.

From the midst of the debacle of Braddock's defeat rises the figure of the young Washington. Twenty-three he was then, tall and spare and hardbodied from a life spent largely in the open. When Braddock fell, this Washington appeared. Reckless of the enemy's bullets, which spanged about him and pierced his clothes, he dashed up and down the lines in an effort to rally the panic-stricken redcoats. He was too late to save the day, but not to save a remnant of the army and bring out his own Virginians in good order. Whether among the stay-at-homes and voters of credits there were some who would have ascribed Washington's conduct on that day to the fact that his brothers were large shareholders in the Ohio Company and that Fort Duquesne was their personal property or "private interest," history does not say. We may suppose so.

North Carolina, the one colony which had not

"amus'd" the Governor of Virginia "with Expectations that proved fruitless," had voted £12,000
for the war and had raised two companies of troops.
One of these, under Edward Brice Dobbs, son of
Governor Dobbs, marched with Braddock; and in
that company as wagoner went Daniel Boone,
then in his twenty-second year. Of Boone's part
in Braddock's campaign nothing more is recorded
save that on the march he made friends with John
Findlay, the trader, his future guide into Kentucky; and that, on the day of the defeat, when his
wagons were surrounded, he escaped by slashing
the harness, leaping on the back of one of his horses,
and dashing into the forest.

Meanwhile the southern tribes along the border
were comparatively quiet. That they well knew
a colossal struggle between the two white races
was pending and were predisposed to ally themselves with the stronger is not to be doubted.
French influence had long been sifting through
the formidable Cherokee nation, which still, however, held true in the main to its treaties with the
English. It was the policy of the Governors of
Virginia and North Carolina to induce the Cherokees to enter strongly into the war as allies of the

English. Their efforts came to nothing chiefly because of the purely local and suicidal Indian policy
of Governor Glen of South Carolina. There had
been some dispute between Glen and Dinwiddie
as to the right of Virginia to trade with the Cherokees; and Glen had sent to the tribes letters cal-
culated to sow distrust of all other aspirants for
Indian favor, even promising that certain settlers
in the Back Country of North Carolina should be
removed and their holdings restored to the Indians.
These letters caused great indignation in North
Carolina, when they came to light, and had the
worst possible effect upon Indian relations. The
Indians now inclined their ear to the French who,
though fewer than the English, were at least united
in purpose.

Governor Glen took this inauspicious moment to
hold high festival with the Cherokees. It was the
last year of his administration and apparently he
hoped to win promotion to some higher post by
showing his achievements for the fur trade and in
the matter of new land acquired. He plied the
Cherokees with drink and induced them to make
formal submission and to cede all their lands to the
Crown. When the chiefs recovered their sobriety,
they were filled with rage at what had been done,

and they remembered how the French had told them that the English intended to make slaves of all the Indians and to steal their lands. The situation was complicated by another incident. Several Cherokee warriors returning from the Ohio, whither they had gone to fight for the British, were slain by frontiersmen. The tribe, in accordance with existing agreements, applied to Virginia for redress — but received none.

There was thus plenty of powder for an explosion. Governor Lyttleton, Glen's successor, at last flung the torch into the magazine. He seized, as hostages, a number of friendly chiefs who were coming to Charleston to offer tokens of good will and forced them to march under guard on a military tour which the Governor was making (1759) with intent to overawe the savages. When this expedition reached Prince George, on the upper waters of the Savannah, the Indian hostages were confined within the fort; and the Governor, satisfied with the result of his maneuver departed south for Charleston. Then followed a tragedy. Some Indian friends of the imprisoned chiefs attacked the fort, and the commander, a popular young officer, was treacherously killed during a parley. The infuriated frontiersmen within the fort fell upon the hostages and slew them all — twenty-six chiefs — and the Indian war was on.

If all were to be told of the struggle which followed in the Back Country, the story could not be contained in this book. Many brave and resourceful men went out against the savages. We can afford only a passing glance at one of them. Hugh Waddell of North Carolina was the most brilliant of all the frontier fighters in that war. He was a young Ulsterman from County Down, a born soldier, with a special genius for fighting Indians, although he did not grow up on the border, for he arrived in North Carolina in 1753, at the age of nineteen. He was appointed by Governor Dobbs to command the second company which North Carolina had raised for the war, a force of 450 rangers to protect the border counties; and he presently became the most conspicuous military figure in the colony. As to his personality, we have only a few meager details, with a portrait that suggests plainly enough those qualities of boldness and craft which characterized his tactics. Governor Dobbs appears to have had a special love towards Hugh, whose family he had known in Ireland, for an undercurrent of almost fatherly pride is to be found in the old Governor's reports to the Assembly concerning Waddell's exploits.

The terror raged for nearly three years. Cabins and fields were burned, and women and children were slaughtered or dragged away captives. Not only did immigration cease but many hardy settlers fled from the country. At length, after horrors indescribable and great toll of life, the Cherokees gave up the struggle. Their towns were invaded and laid waste by imperial and colonial troops, and they could do nothing but make peace. In 1761 they signed a treaty with the English to hold "while rivers flow and grasses grow and sun and moon endure."

In the previous year (1760) the imperial war had run its course in America. New France lay prostrate, and the English were supreme not only on the Ohio but on the St. Lawrence and the Great Lakes. Louisbourg, Quebec, Montreal, Oswego, Niagara, Duquesne, Detroit — all were in English hands.

Hugh Waddell and his rangers, besides serving with distinction in the Indian war, had taken part in the capture of Fort Duquesne. This feat had been accomplished in 1758 by an expedition under General Forbes. The troops made a terrible march over a new route, cutting a road as they went. It was November when they approached their objective. The wastes of snow and their diminished supplies caused such depression among the men that the officers called a halt to discuss whether or not to proceed toward Fort Duquesne, where they believed the French to be concentrated in force. Extravagant sums in guineas were named as suitable reward for any man who would stalk and catch a French Indian and learn from him the real conditions inside the fort. The honor, if not the guineas, fell to John Rogers, one of Waddell's rangers. From the Indian it was learned that the French had already gone, leaving behind only a few of their number. As the English drew near, they found that the garrison had blown up the magazine, set fire to the fort, and made off.

Thus, while New France was already tottering, but nearly two years before the final capitulation at Montreal, the English again became masters of the Ohio Company's land — masters of the Forks of the Ohio. This time they were there to stay. Where the walls of Fort Duquesne had crumbled in the fire Fort Pitt was to rise, proudly bearing the name of England's Great Commoner who had directed English arms to victory on three continents.

With France expelled and the Indians deprived

of their white allies, the westward path lay open to the pioneers, even though the red man himself would rise again and again in vain endeavor to bar the way. So a new era begins, the era of exploration for definite purpose, the era of commonwealth building. In entering on it, we part with the earliest pioneer — the trader, who first opened the road for both the lone home seeker and the great land company. He dwindles now to the mere barterer and so — save for a few chance glimpses — slips out of sight, for his brave days as Imperial Scout are done.

CHAPTER V

BOONE, THE WANDERER

WHAT thoughts filled Daniel Boone's mind as he was returning from Braddock's disastrous campaign in 1755 we may only conjecture. Perhaps he was planning a career of soldiering, for in later years he was to distinguish himself as a frontier commander in both defense and attack. Or it may be that his heart was full of the wondrous tales told him by the trader, John Findlay, of that Hunter's Canaan, Kentucky, where buffalo and deer roamed in thousands. Perhaps he meant to set out ere long in search of the great adventure of his dreams, despite the terrible dangers of trail making across the zones of war into the unknown.

However that may be, Boone straightway followed neither of these possible plans on his return to the Yadkin but halted for a different adventure. There, a rifle shot's distance from his threshold, was offered him the oldest and sweetest of all hazards to the daring. He was twenty-two, strong and comely and a whole man; and therefore he was in no mind to refuse what life held out to him in the person of Rebecca Bryan. Rebecca was the daughter of Joseph Bryan, who had come to the Yadkin from Pennsylvania some time before the Boones; and she was in her seventeenth year.

Writers of an earlier and more sentimental period than ours have endeavored to supply, from the saccharine stores of their fancy, the romantic episodes connected with Boone's wooing which history has omitted to record. Hence the tale that the young hunter, walking abroad in the spring gloaming, saw Mistress Rebecca's large dark eyes shining in the dusk of the forest, mistook them for a deer's eyes and shot — his aim on this occasion fortunately being bad! But if Boone's rifle was missing its mark at ten paces, Cupid's dart was speeding home. So runs the story concocted a hundred years later by some gentle scribe ignorant alike of game seasons, the habits of hunters, and the way of a man with a maid in a primitive world.

Daniel and Rebecca were married in the spring of 1756. Squire Boone, in his capacity as justice of the peace, tied the knot; and in a small cabin built upon his spacious lands the young couple

set up housekeeping.   Here Daniel's first two sons
were born.   In the third year of his marriage, when
the second child was a babe in arms, Daniel removed with his wife and their young and precious
family to Culpeper County in eastern Virginia, for
the border was going through its darkest days of
the French and Indian War.   During the next two
or three years we find him in Virginia engaged
as a wagoner, hauling tobacco in season; but back
on the border with his rifle, after the harvest,
aiding in defense against the Indians.   In 1759 he
purchased from his father a lot on Sugar Tree Creek,
a tributary of Dutchman's Creek (Davie County,
North Carolina) and built thereon a cabin for himself.   The date when he brought his wife and children to live in their new abode on the border is
not recorded.   It was probably some time after
the close of the Indian War.   Of Boone himself
during these years we have but scant information.   We hear of him again in Virginia and also as
a member of the pack-horse caravan which brought
into the Back Country the various necessaries for
the settlers.   We know, too, that in the fall of 1760
he was on a lone hunting trip in the mountains
west of the Yadkin; for until a few years ago
there might be seen, still standing on the banks

of Boone's Creek (a small tributary of the Watauga) in eastern Tennessee, a tree bearing the legend, "D Boon cilled A BAR on this tree 1760." Boone was always fond of carving his exploits on trees, and his wanderings have been traced largely by his arboreal publications. In the next year (1761) he went with Waddell's rangers when they marched with the army to the final subjugation of the Cherokee.

That Boone and his family were back on the border in the new cabin shortly after the end of the war, we gather from the fact that in 1764 he took his little son James, aged seven, on one of his long hunting excursions. From this time dates the intimate comradeship of father and son through all the perils of the wilderness, a comradeship to come to its tragic end ten years later when, as we shall see, the seventeen-year-old lad fell under the red man's tomahawk as his father was leading the first settlers towards Kentucky. In the cold nights of the open camp, as Daniel and James lay under the frosty stars, the father kept the boy warm snuggled to his breast under the broad flap of his hunting shirt. Sometimes the two were away from home for months together, and Daniel declared little James to be as good a woodsman as his father.

Meanwhile fascinating accounts of the new land of Florida, ceded to Britain by the Treaty of Paris in 1763, had leaked into the Back Country; and in the winter of 1765 Boone set off southward on horseback with seven companions. Colonel James Grant, with whose army Boone had fought in 1761, had been appointed Governor of the new colony and was offering generous inducements to settlers. The party traveled along the borders of South Carolina and Georgia. No doubt they made the greater part of their way over the old Traders' Trace, the "whitened" warpath; and they suffered severe hardships. Game became scarcer as they proceeded. Once they were nigh to perishing of starvation and were saved from that fate only through chance meeting with a band of Indians who, seeing their plight, made camp and shared their food with them — according to the Indian code in time of peace.

Boone's party explored Florida from St. Augustine to Pensacola, and Daniel became sufficiently enamored of the tropical south to purchase there land and a house. His wife, however, was unwilling to go to Florida, and she was not long in convincing the hunter that he would soon tire of a gameless country. A gameless country! Perhaps

this was the very thought which turned the wanderer's desires again towards the land of Kentucky.[1]
The silencing of the enemy's whisper in the Cherokee camps had opened the border forests once more
to the nomadic rifleman. Boone was not alone in the
desire to seek out what lay beyond. His brother-in-
law, John Stewart, and a nephew by marriage, Benjamin Cutbirth, or Cutbird, with two other young
men, John Baker and James Ward, in 1766 crossed
the Appalachian Mountains, probably by stumbling
upon the Indian trail winding from base to summit
and from peak to base again over this part of the
great hill barrier. They eventually reached the Mississippi River and, having taken a good quantity of
peltry on the way, they launched upon the stream
and came in time to New Orleans, where they made
a satisfactory trade of their furs.

Boone was fired anew by descriptions of this
successful feat, in which two of his kinsmen had
participated. He could no longer be held back.
He must find the magic door that led through the
vast mountain wall into Kentucky — Kentucky,
with its green prairies where the buffalo and deer

[1] Kentucky, from Ken-ta-ke, an Iroquois word meaning "the place
of old fields." Adair calls the territory "the old fields." The Indians
apparently used the word "old," as we do, in a sense of endearment
and possession as well as relative to age.

were as "ten thousand thousand cattle feeding" in the wilds, and where the balmy air vibrated with the music of innumerable wings.

Accordingly, in the autumn of 1767, Boone began his quest of the delectable country in the company of his friend, William Hill, who had been with him in Florida. Autumn was the season of departure on all forest excursions, because by that time the summer crops had been gathered in and the day of the deer had come. By hunting, the explorers must feed themselves on their travels and with deerskins and furs they must on their return recompense those who had supplied their outfit. Boone, the incessant but not always lucky wanderer, was in these years ever in debt for an outfit.

Boone and Hill made their way over the Blue Ridge and the Alleghanies and crossed the Holston and Clinch rivers. Then they came upon the west fork of the Big Sandy and, believing that it would lead them to the Ohio, they continued for at least a hundred miles to the westward. Here they found a buffalo trace, one of the many beaten out by the herds in their passage to the salt springs, and they followed it into what is now Floyd County in eastern Kentucky. But this was not the prairie land described by Findlay; it was rough and hilly and so overgrown with laurel as to be almost impenetrable. They therefore wended their way back towards the river, doubtless erected the usual hunter's camp of skins or blankets and branches, and spent the winter in hunting and trapping. Spring found them returning to their homes on the Yadkin with a fair winter's haul.

Such urgent desire as Boone's, however, was not to be defeated. The next year brought him his great opportunity. John Findlay came to the Yadkin with a horse pack of needles and linen and peddler's wares to tempt the slim purses of the Back Country folk. The two erstwhile comrades in arms were overjoyed to encounter each other again, and Findlay spent the winter of 1768–69 in Boone's cabin. While the snow lay deep outside and good-smelling logs crackled on the hearth, they planned an expedition into Kentucky through the Gap where Virginia, Tennessee, and Kentucky touch one another, which Findlay felt confident he could find. Findlay had learned of this route from cross-mountain traders in 1753, when he had descended the Ohio to the site of Louisville, whence he had gone with some Shawanoes as a prisoner to their town of Es-kip-pa-ki-thi-ki or Blue Licks.[1]

[1] Hanna, *The Wilderness Trail*, vol. ii, pp. 215–16.

7

On the first day of May, 1769, Boone and Findlay, accompanied by John Stewart and three other venturesome spirits, Joseph Holden, James Mooney, and William Cooley, took horse for the fabled land. Passing through the Cumberland Gap, they built their first camp in Kentucky on the Red Lick fork of Station Camp Creek.

This camp was their base of operations. From it, usually in couples, we infer, the explorers branched out to hunt and to take their observations of the country. Here also they prepared the deer and buffalo meat for the winter, dried or smoked the geese they shot in superabundance, made the tallow and oil needed to keep their weapons in trim, their leather soft, and their kits waterproof. Their first ill luck befell them in December when Boone and Stewart were captured by a band of Shawanoes who were returning from their autumn hunt on Green River. The Indians compelled the two white men to show them the location of their camp, took possession of all it contained in skins and furs and also helped themselves to the horses. They left the explorers with just enough meat and ammunition to provide for their journey homeward, and told them to depart and not to intrude again on the red men's hunting grounds. Having given this pointed warning, the Shawanoes rode on northward towards their towns beyond the Ohio. On foot, swiftly and craftily, Boone and his brother-in-law trailed the band for two days. They came upon the camp in dead of night, recaptured their horses, and fled. But this was a game in which the Indians themselves excelled, and at this date the Shawanoes had an advantage over Boone in their thorough knowledge of the territory; so that within forty-eight hours the white men were once more prisoners. After they had amused themselves by making Boone caper about with a horse bell on his neck, while they jeered at him in broken English, "Steal horse, eh?" the Shawanoes turned north again, this time taking the two unfortunate hunters with them. Boone and Stewart escaped, one day on the march, by a plunge into the thick tall canebrake. Though the Indians did not attempt to follow them through the mazes of the cane, the situation of the two hunters, without weapons or food, was serious enough. When they found Station Camp deserted and realized that their four companions had given them up for dead or lost and had set off on the trail for home, even such intrepid souls as theirs may have felt fear. They raced on in pursuit and fortunately fell in not only with their party but with Squire Boone, Daniel's brother, and Alexander Neely, who had brought in fresh supplies of rifles, ammunition, flour, and horses.

After this lucky encounter the group separated. Findlay was ill, and Holden, Mooney, and Cooley had had their fill of Kentucky; but Squire, Neely, Stewart, and Daniel were ready for more adventures. Daniel, too, felt under the positive necessity of putting in another year at hunting and trapping in order to discharge his debts and provide for his family. Near the mouth of Red River the new party built their station camp. Here, in idle hours, Neely read aloud from a copy of *Gulliver's Travels* to entertain the hunters while they dressed their deerskins or tinkered their weapons. In honor of the "Lorbrulgrud" of the book, though with a pronunciation all their own, they christened the nearest creek; and as "Lulbegrud Creek" it is still known.

Before the end of the winter the two Boones were alone in the wilderness. Their brother-in-law, Stewart, had disappeared; and Neely, discouraged by this tragic event, had returned to the Yadkin. In May, Squire Boone fared forth, taking with him the season's catch of beaver, otter, and deerskins to exchange in the North Carolinian trading houses for more supplies; and Daniel was left solitary in Kentucky.

Now followed those lonely explorations which gave Daniel Boone his special fame above all Kentucky's pioneers. He was by no means the first white man to enter Kentucky; and when he did enter, it was as one of a party, under another man's guidance — if we except his former disappointing journey into the laurel thickets of Floyd County. But these others, barring Stewart, who fell there, turned back when they met with loss and hardship and measured the certain risks against the possible gains. Boone, the man of imagination, turned to wild earth as to his kin. His genius lay in the sense of oneness he felt with his wilderness environment. An instinct he had which these other men, as courageous perhaps as he, did not possess.

Never in all the times when he was alone in the woods and had no other man's safety or counsel to consider, did he suffer ill fortune. The nearest approach to trouble that befell him when alone occurred one day during this summer when some Indians emerged from their green shelter and found him, off guard for the moment, standing on a cliff gazing with rapture over the vast rolling stretches of Kentucky. He was apparently cut off from escape, for the savages were on three sides, advancing without haste to take him, meanwhile greeting him with mock amity. Over the cliff leaped Boone and into the outspread arms of a friendly maple, whose top bloomed green about sixty feet below the cliff's rim, and left his would-be captors on the height above, grunting their amazement.

During this summer Boone journeyed through the valleys of the Kentucky and the Licking. He followed the buffalo traces to the two Blue Licks and saw the enormous herds licking up the salt earth, a darkly ruddy moving mass of beasts whose numbers could not be counted. For many miles he wound along the Ohio, as far as the Falls. He also found the Big Bone Lick with its mammoth fossils.

In July, 1770, Daniel returned to the Red River camp and there met Squire Boone with another pack of supplies. The two brothers continued their hunting and exploration together for some months, chiefly in Jessamine County, where two caves still bear Boone's name. In that winter they even braved the Green River ground, whence had come the hunting Shawanoes who had taken Daniel's first fruits a year before. In the same year (1770) there had come into Kentucky from the Yadkin another party of hunters, called, from their lengthy sojourn in the twilight zone, the Long Hunters. One of these, Gasper Mansker, afterwards related how the Long Hunters were startled one day by hearing sounds such as no buffalo or turkey ever made, and how Mansker himself stole silently under cover of the trees towards the place whence the strange noises came, and descried Daniel Boone prone on his back with a deerskin under him, his famous tall black hat beside him and his mouth opened wide in joyous but apparently none too tuneful song. This incident gives a true character touch. It is not recorded of any of the men who turned back that they sang alone in the wilderness.

In March, 1771, the two Boones started homeward, their horses bearing the rich harvest of furs and deerskins which was to clear Daniel of debt and to insure the comfort of the family he had not seen for two years. But again evil fortune met them, this time in the very gates — for in the Cumberland Gap they were suddenly surrounded by Indians who took everything from them, leaving them neither guns nor horses.

CHAPTER VI

THE FIGHT FOR KENTUCKY

When Boone returned home he found the Back Country of North Carolina in the throes of the Regulation Movement. This movement, which had arisen first from the colonists' need to police their settlements, had more recently assumed a political character. The Regulators were now in conflict with the authorities, because the frontier folk were suffering through excessive taxes, extortionate fees, dishonest land titles, and the corruption of the courts. In May, 1771, the conflict lost its quasi-civil nature. The Regulators resorted to arms and were defeated by the forces under Governor Tryon in the Battle of the Alamance.

The Regulation Movement, which we shall follow in more detail further on, was a culmination of those causes of unrest which turned men westward. To escape from oppression and to acquire land beyond the bounds of tyranny became the earnest desire of independent spirits throughout the Back Country. But there was another and more potent reason why the country east of the mountains no longer contented Boone. Hunting and trapping were Boone's chief means of livelihood. In those days, deerskins sold for a dollar a skin to the traders at the Forks or in Hillsborough; beaver at about two dollars and a half, and otter at from three to five dollars. A pack-horse could carry a load of one hundred dressed deerskins, and, as currency was scarce, a hundred dollars was wealth. Game was fast disappearing from the Yadkin. To Boone above all men, then, Kentucky beckoned. When he returned in the spring of 1771 from his explorations, it was with the resolve to take his family at once into the great game country and to persuade some of his friends to join in this hazard of new fortunes.

The perils of such a venture, only conjectural to us at this distance, he knew well; but in him there was nothing that shrank from danger, though he did not court it after the rash manner of many of his compeers. Neither reckless nor riotous, Boone was never found among those who opposed violence to authority, even unjust authority; nor was he ever guilty of the savagery which characterized much of the retaliatory warfare of that period when frenzied white men bettered the red man's instruction. In him, courage was illumined with tenderness and made equable by self-control. Yet, though he was no fiery zealot like the Ulstermen who were to follow him along the path he had made and who loved and revered him perhaps because he was so different from themselves, Boone nevertheless had his own religion. It was a simple faith best summed up perhaps by himself in his old age when he said that he had been only an instrument in the hand of God to open the wilderness to settlement.

Two years passed before Boone could muster a company of colonists for the dangerous and delectable land. The dishonesty practiced by Lord Granville's agents in the matter of deeds had made it difficult for Daniel and his friends to dispose of their acreage. When at last in the spring of 1773 the Wanderer was prepared to depart, he was again delayed; this time by the arrival of a little son to whom was given the name of John. By September, however, even this latest addition to the party was ready for travel; and that month saw the Boones with a small caravan of families journeying towards Powell's Valley, whence the

Warrior's Path took its way through Cumberland Gap. At this point on the march they were to be joined by William Russell, a famous pioneer, from the Clinch River, with his family and a few neighbors, and by some of Rebecca Boone's kinsmen, the Bryans, from the lower Yadkin, with a company of forty men.

Of Rebecca Boone history tells us too little — only that she was born a Bryan, was of low stature and dark eyed, that she bore her husband ten children, and lived beside him to old age. Except on his hunts and explorations, she went with him from one cabined home to another, always deeper into the wilds. There are no portraits of her. We can see her only as a shadowy figure moving along the wilderness trails beside the man who accepted his destiny of God to be a way-shower for those of lesser faith.

He tires not forever on his leagues of march
Because her feet are set to his footprints,
And the gleam of her bare hand slants across his
    shoulder.

Boone halted his company on Walden Mountain over Powell's Valley to await the Bryan contingent and dispatched two young men under the leadership of his son James, then in his seventeenth year, to notify Russell of the party's arrival. As the boys were returning with Russell's son, also a stripling, two of his slaves, and some white laborers, they missed the path and went into camp for the night. When dawn broke, disclosing the sleepers, a small war band of Shawanoes, who had been spying on Boone and his party, fell upon them and slaughtered them. Only one of Russell's slaves and a laborer escaped. The tragedy seems augmented by the fact that the point where the boys lost the trail and made their night quarters was hardly three miles from the main camp — to which an hour later came the two survivors with their gloomy tidings. Terror now took hold of the little band of emigrants, and there were loud outcries for turning back. The Bryans, who had arrived meanwhile, also advised retreat, saying that the "signs" about the scene of blood indicated an Indian uprising. Daniel carried the scalped body of his son, the boy-comrade of his happy hunts, to the camp and buried it there at the beginning of the trail. His voice alone urged that they go on.

Fortunately indeed, as events turned out, Boone was overruled, and the expedition was abandoned. The Bryan party and the others from North Carolina went back to the Yadkin. Boone himself with his family accompanied Russell to the Clinch settlement, where he erected a temporary cabin on the farm of one of the settlers, and then set out alone on the chase to earn provision for his wife and children through the winter.

Those who prophesied an Indian war were not mistaken. When the snowy hunting season had passed and the "Powwowing Days" were come, the Indian war drum rattled in the medicine house from the borders of Pennsylvania to those of Carolina. The causes of the strife for which the red men were making ready must be briefly noted to help us form a just opinion of the deeds that followed. Early writers have usually represented the frontiersmen as saints in buckskin and the Indians as fiends without the shadow of a claim on either the land or humanity. Many later writers have merely reversed the shield. The truth is that the Indians and the borderers reacted upon each other to the hurt of both. Paradoxically, they grew like enough to hate one another with a savage hatred — and both wanted the land.

Land! Land! was the slogan of all sorts and conditions of men. Tidewater officials held solemn powwows with the chiefs, gave wampum strings, and forthwith incorporated.[1] Chiefs blessed their white brothers who had "forever brightened the chain of friendship," departed home, and proceeded to brighten the blades of their tomahawks and to await, not long, the opportunity to use them on casual hunters who carried in their kits the compass, the "land-stealer." Usually the surveying hunter was a borderer; and on him the tomahawk descended with an accelerated gusto. Private citizens also formed land companies and sent out surveyors, regardless of treaties. Bold frontiersmen went into No Man's Land and staked out their claims. In the very year when disaster turned the Boone party back, James Harrod had entered Kentucky from Pennsylvania and had marked the site of a settlement.

Ten years earlier (1763), the King had issued the famous and much misunderstood Proclamation restricting his "loving subjects" from the lands west of the mountains. The colonists interpreted this document as a tyrannous curtailment of their liberties for the benefit of the fur trade. We know now that the portion of this Proclamation relating to western settlement was a wise provision

---

[1] The activities of the great land companies are described in Alvord's exhaustive work, *The Mississippi Valley in British Politics.*

designed to protect the settlers on the frontier by allaying the suspicions of the Indians, who viewed with apprehension the triumphal occupation of that vast territory from Canada to the Gulf of Mexico by the colonizing English. By seeking to compel all land purchase to be made through the Crown, it was designed likewise to protect the Indians from "whisky purchase," and to make impossible the transfer of their lands except with consent of the Indian Council, or full quota of headmen, whose joint action alone conveyed what the tribes considered to be legal title. Sales made according to this form, Sir William Johnson declared to the Lords of Trade, he had never known to be repudiated by the Indians. This paragraph of the Proclamation was in substance an embodiment of Johnson's suggestions to the Lords of Trade. Its purpose was square dealing and pacification; and shrewd men such as Washington recognized that it was not intended as a final check to expansion. "A temporary expedient to quiet the minds of the Indians," Washington called it, and then himself went out along the Great Kanawha and into Kentucky, surveying land.

It will be asked what had become of the Ohio Company of Virginia and that fort at the Forks of the Ohio, once a bone of contention between France and England. Fort Pitt, as it was now called, had fallen foul of another dispute, this time between Virginia and Pennsylvania. Virginia claimed that the far western corner of her boundary ascended just far enough north to take in Fort Pitt. Pennsylvania asserted that it did nothing of the sort. The Ohio Company had meanwhile been merged into the Walpole Company. George Croghan, at Fort Pitt, was the Company's agent and as such was accused by Pennsylvania of favoring from ulterior motives the claims of Virginia. Hotheads in both colonies asseverated that the Indians were secretly being stirred up in connection with the boundary disputes. If it does not very clearly appear how an Indian rising would have settled the ownership of Fort Pitt, it is evident enough where the interests of Virginia and Pennsylvania clashed. Virginia wanted land for settlement and speculation; Pennsylvania wanted the Indians left in possession for the benefit of the fur trade. So far from stirring up the Indians, as his enemies declared, Croghan was as usual giving away all his substance to keep them quiet.[1] Indeed,

[1] The suspicion that Croghan and Lord Dunmore, the Governor of Virginia, were instigating the war appears to have arisen out of the

during this summer of 1774, eleven hundred Indians
were encamped about Fort Pitt visiting him.

Two hundred thousand acres in the West —
Kentucky and West Virginia — had been promised
to the colonial officers and soldiers who fought
in the Seven Years' War. But after making the
Proclamation the British Government had delayed
issuing the patents. Washington interested himself in trying to secure them; and Lord Dunmore,
who also had caught the "land-fever,"[1] prodded
the British authorities but won only rebuke for
his inconvenient activities. Insistent, however,
Dunmore sent out parties of surveyors to fix the
bounds of the soldiers' claims. James Harrod, Captain Thomas Bullitt, Hancock Taylor, and three
McAfee brothers entered Kentucky, by the Ohio,
under Dunmore's orders. John Floyd went in by

conduct of Dr. John Connolly, Dunmore's agent and Croghan's
nephew. Croghan had induced the Shawanoes to bring under escort
to Fort Pitt certain English traders resident in the Indian towns. The
escort was fired on by militiamen under command of Connolly, who
also issued a proclamation declaring a state of war to exist. Connolly,
however, probably acted on his own initiative. He was interested
in land on his own behalf and was by no means the only man at that
time who was ready to commit outrages on Indians in order to obtain
it. As Croghan lamented, there was "too great a spirit in the frontier
people for killing Indians."

[1] See Alvord, *The Mississippi Valley in British Politics*, vol. II, pp.
191–94.

the Kanawha as Washington's agent. A bird's-eye view of that period would disclose to us very few indeed of His Majesty's loving subjects who were paying any attention to his proclamation. Early in 1774, Harrod began the building of cabins and a fort, and planted corn on the site of Harrodsburg. Thus to him and not to Boone fell the honor of founding the first permanent white settlement in Kentucky

When summer came, its thick verdure proffering ambuscade, the air hung tense along the border. Traders had sent in word that Shawanoes, Delawares, Mingos, Wyandots, and Cherokees were refusing all other exchange than rifles, ammunition, knives, and hatchets. White men were shot down in their fields from ambush. Dead Indians lay among their own young corn, their scalp locks taken. There were men of both races who wanted war and meant to have it — and with it the land.

Lord Dunmore, the Governor, resolved that, if war were inevitable, it should be fought out in the Indian country. With this intent, he wrote to Colonel Andrew Lewis of Botetourt County, Commander of the Southwest Militia, instructing him to raise a respectable body of troops and "join me either at the mouth of the Great Kanawha or Wheeling, or such other part of the Ohio as may be most convenient for you to meet me." The Governor himself with a force of twelve hundred proceeded to Fort Pitt, where Croghan, as we have seen, was extending his hospitality to eleven hundred warriors from the disaffected tribes.

On receipt of the Governor's letter, Andrew Lewis sent out expresses to his brother Colonel Charles Lewis, County Lieutenant of Augusta, and to Colonel William Preston, County Lieutenant of Fincastle, to raise men and bring them with all speed to the rendezvous at Camp Union (Lewisburg) on the Big Levels of the Greenbrier (West Virginia). Andrew Lewis summoned these officers to an expedition for "reducing our inveterate enemies to reason." Preston called for volunteers to take advantage of "the opportunity we have so long wished for . . . this useless People may now at last be Oblidged to abandon their country." These men were among not only the bravest but the best of their time; but this was their view of the Indian and his alleged rights. To eliminate this "useless people," inveterate enemies of the white race, was, as they saw it, a political necessity and a religious duty. And we today who profit by their deeds dare not condemn them.

Fervor less solemn was aroused in other quarters by Dunmore's call to arms. At Wheeling, some eighty or ninety young adventurers, in charge of Captain Michael Cresap of Maryland, were waiting for the freshets to sweep them down the Ohio into Kentucky. When the news reached them, they greeted it with the wild monotone chant and the ceremonies preliminary to Indian warfare. They planted the war pole, stripped and painted themselves, and starting the war dance called on Cresap to be their "white leader." The captain, however, declined; but in that wild circling line was one who was a white leader indeed. He was a sandy-haired boy of twenty — one of the bold race of English Virginians, rugged and of fiery countenance, with blue eyes intense of glance and deep set under a high brow that, while modeled for power, seemed threatened in its promise by the too sensitive chiseling of his lips. With every nerve straining for the fray, with thudding of feet and crooning of the blood song, he wheeled with those other mad spirits round the war pole till the set of sun closed the rites. "That evening two scalps were brought into camp," so a letter of his reads.

Does the bold savage color of this picture affright us? Would we veil it? Then we should lose something of the true lineaments of George Rogers Clark, who, within four short years, was to lead a tiny army of tattered and starving backwoodsmen, ashamed to quail where he never flinched, through barrens and icy floods to the conquest of Illinois for the United States.

Though Cresap had rejected the rôle of "white leader," he did not escape the touch of infamy. "Cresap's War" was the name the Indians gave to the bloody encounters between small parties of whites and Indians, which followed on that war dance and scalping, during the summer months. One of these encounters must be detailed here because history has assigned it as the immediate cause of Dunmore's War.

Greathouse, Sapperton, and King, three traders who had a post on Yellow Creek, a tributary of the Ohio fifty miles below Pittsburgh, invited several Indians from across the stream to come and drink with them and their friends. Among the Indians were two or three men of importance in the Mingo tribe. There were also some women, one of whom was the Indian wife of Colonel John Gibson, an educated man who had distinguished himself as a soldier with Forbes in 1758. That the Indians came in amity and apprehended no treachery was proved by the presence of the women. Gibson's wife carried her half-caste baby in her shawl. The disreputable traders plied their guests with drink to the point of intoxication and then murdered them. King shot the first man and, when he fell, cut his throat, saying that he had served many a deer in that fashion. Gibson's Indian wife fled and was shot down in the clearing. A man followed to dispatch her and her baby. She held the child up to him pleading, with her last breath, that he would spare it because it was not Indian but "one of yours." The mother dead, the child was later sent to Gibson. Twelve Indians in all were killed.

Meanwhile Croghan had persuaded the Iroquois to peace. With the help of David Zeisberger, the Moravian missionary, and White Eyes, a Delaware chief, he and Dunmore had won over the Delaware warriors. In the Cherokee councils, Oconostota demanded that the treaty of peace signed in 1761 be kept. The Shawanoes, however, led by Cornstalk, were implacable; and they had as allies the Ottawas and Mingos, who had entered the council with them.

A famous chief of the day and one of great influence over the Indians, and also among the white officials who dealt with Indian affairs, was Tach-nech-dor-us, or Branching Oak of the Forest, a Mingo who had taken the name of Logan out of compliment to James Logan of Pennsylvania. Chief Logan had recently met with so much reproach from his red brothers for his loyalty to the whites that he had departed from the Mingo town at Yellow Creek. But, learning that his tribe had determined to assist the Shawanoes and had already taken some white scalps, he repaired to the place where the Mingos were holding their war council to exert his powers for peace. There, in presence of the warriors, after swaying them from their purpose by those oratorical gifts which gave him his influence and his renown, he took the war hatchet that had already killed, and buried it in proof that vengeance was appeased. Upon this scene there entered a Mingo from Yellow Creek with the news of the murders committed there by the three traders. The Indian whose throat had been slit as King had served deer was Logan's brother. Another man slain was his kinsman. The woman with the baby was his sister. Logan tore up from the earth the bloody tomahawk and, raising it above his head, swore that he would not rest till he had taken ten white lives to pay for each one of his kin. Again the Mingo warriors declared for war and this time were not dissuaded. But Logan did not join this red army. He went out alone to wreak his vengeance, slaying and scalping.

Meanwhile Dunmore prepared to push the war with the utmost vigor. His first concern was to recall the surveying parties from Kentucky, and for so hazardous an errand he needed the services of a man whose endurance, speed, and woodcraft were equal to those of any Indian scout afoot. Through Colonel Preston, his orders were conveyed to Daniel Boone, for Boone's fame had now spread from the border to the tidewater regions. It was stated that "Boone would lose no time," and "if they are alive, it is indisputable but Boone must find them."

So Boone set out in company with Michael Stoner, another expert woodsman. His general instructions were to go down the Kentucky River to Preston's Salt Lick and across country to the Falls of the Ohio, and thence home by Gaspar's Lick on the Cumberland River. Indian war parties were moving under cover across "the Dark and Bloody Ground" to surround the various groups of surveyors still at large and to exterminate them. Boone made his journey successfully. He found John Floyd, who was surveying for Washington; he sped up to where Harrod and his band were building cabins and sent them out, just in time as it happened; he reached all the outposts of Thomas Bullitt's party, only one of whom fell a victim to the foe[1]; and, undetected by the Indians, he brought himself and Stoner home in safety, after covering eight hundred miles in sixty-one days.

Harrod and his homesteaders immediately enlisted in the army. How eager Boone was to go with the forces under Lewis is seen in the official correspondence relative to Dunmore's War. Floyd wanted Boone's help in raising a company: "Captain Bledsoe says that Boone has more [influence] than any man now disengaged; and you know what Boone has done for me . . . for which reason I love the man." Even the border, it would seem, had its species of pacifists who were willing to let others take risks for them, for men hung back from recruiting, and desertions were the order of the day. Major Arthur Campbell hit upon a solution

[1] Hancock Taylor, who delayed in getting out of the country and was cut off.

of the difficulties in West Fincastle. He was convinced that Boone could raise a company and hold the men loyal. And Boone did.

For some reason, however, Daniel's desire to march with the army was denied. Perhaps it was because just such a man as he — and, indeed, there was no other — was needed to guard the settlement. Presently he was put in command of Moore's Fort in Clinch Valley, and his "diligence" received official approbation. A little later the inhabitants of the valley sent out a petition to have Boone made a "captain" and given supreme command of the lower forts. The settlers demanded Boone's promotion for their own security.

> The land it is good, it is just to our mind,
> Each will have his part if his Lordship be kind,
> The Ohio once ours, we'll live at our ease,
> With a bottle and glass to drink when we please.

So sang the army poet, thus giving voice, as bards should ever do, to the theme nearest the hearts of his hearers — in this case, Land! Presumably his ditty was composed on the eve of the march from Lewisburg, for it is found in a soldier's diary.

On the evening of October 9, 1774, Andrew Lewis with his force of eleven hundred frontiersmen was encamped on Point Pleasant at the junction of the Great Kanawha with the Ohio. Dunmore in the meantime had led his forces into Ohio and had erected Fort Gower at the mouth of the Hockhocking River, where he waited for word from Andrew Lewis.[1]

The movements of the two armies were being observed by scouts from the force of red warriors gathered in Ohio under the great leader of the Shawanoes. Cornstalk purposed to isolate the two armies of his enemy and to crush them in turn before they could come together. His first move was to launch an attack on Lewis at Point

[1] It has been customary to ascribe to Lord Dunmore motives of treachery in failing to make connections with Lewis; but no real evidence has been advanced to support any of the charges made against him by local historians. The charges were, as Theodore Roosevelt says, "an afterthought." Dunmore was a King's man in the Revolution; and yet in March, 1775, the Convention of the Colony of Virginia, assembled in opposition to the royal party, resolved: "The most cordial thanks of the people of this colony are a tribute justly due to our worthy Governor, Lord Dunmore, for his truly noble, wise, and spirited conduct which at once evinces his Excellency's attention to the true interests of this colony, and a zeal in the executive department which no dangers can divert, or difficulties hinder, from achieving the most important services to the people who have the happiness to live under his administration." (See *American Archives*, Fourth Series, vol. II, p. 170.) Similar resolutions were passed by his officers on the march home from Ohio; at the same time, the officers passed resolutions in sympathy with the American cause. Yet it was Andrew Lewis who later drove Dunmore from Virginia. Well might Dunmore exclaim, "That it should ever come to this!"

Pleasant. In the dark of night, Cornstalk's Indians crossed the Ohio on rafts, intending to surprise the white man's camp at dawn. They would have succeeded but for the chance that three or four of the frontiersmen, who had risen before daybreak to hunt, came upon the Indians creeping towards the camp. Shots were exchanged. An Indian and a white man dropped. The firing roused the camp. Three hundred men in two lines under Charles Lewis and William Fleming sallied forth expecting to engage the vanguard of the enemy but encountered almost the whole force of from eight hundred to a thousand Indians before the rest of the army could come into action. Both officers were wounded, Charles Lewis fatally. The battle, which continued from dawn until an hour before sunset, was the bloodiest in Virginia's long series of Indian wars. The frontiersmen fought as such men ever fought — with the daring, bravery, swiftness of attack, and skill in taking cover which were the tactics of their day, even as at a later time many of these same men fought at King's Mountain and in Illinois the battles that did so much to turn the tide in the Revolution.[1]

[1] With Andrew Lewis on this day were Isaac Shelby and William Campbell, the victorious leaders at King's Mountain, James

Colonel Preston wrote to Patrick Henry that the enemy behaved with "inconceivable bravery," the head men walking about in the time of action exhorting their men to "lie close, shoot well, be strong, and fight." The Shawanoes ran up to the muzzles of the English guns, disputing every foot of ground. Both sides knew well what they were fighting for — the rich land held in a semicircle by the Beautiful River.

Shortly before sundown the Indians, mistaking a flank movement by Shelby's contingent for the arrival of reinforcements, retreated across the Ohio. Many of their most noted warriors had fallen and among them the Shawano chief, Puck-e-shin-wa, father of a famous son, Tecumseh.[1] Yet they were unwilling to accept defeat. When they heard that Dunmore was now marching overland to cut them off from their towns, their fury blazed anew. "Shall we first kill all our women and children and then

Robertson, the "father of Tennessee," Valentine Sevier, Daniel Morgan, hero of the Cowpens, Major Arthur Campbell, Benjamin Logan, Anthony Bledsoe, and Simon Kenton. With Dunmore's force were Adam Stephen, who distinguished himself at the Brandywine, George Rogers Clark, John Stuart, already noted through the Cherokee wars, and John Montgomery, later one of Clark's four captains in Illinois. The two last mentioned were Highlanders. Clark's Illinois force was largely recruited from the troops who fought at Point Pleasant.

[1] Thwaites, *Documentary History of Dunmore's War.*

fight till we ourselves are slain?" Cornstalk, in irony, demanded of them; "No? Then I will go and make peace."

By the treaty compacted between the chiefs and Lord Dunmore, the Indians gave up all claim to the lands south of the Ohio, even for hunting, and agreed to allow boats to pass unmolested. In this treaty the Mingos refused to join, and a detachment of Dunmore's troops made a punitive expedition to their towns. Some discord arose between Dunmore and Lewis's frontier forces because, since the Shawanoes had made peace, the Governor would not allow the frontiersmen to destroy the Shawano towns.

Of all the chiefs, Logan alone still held aloof. Major Gibson undertook to fetch him, but Logan refused to come to the treaty grounds. He sent by Gibson the short speech which has lived as an example of the best Indian oratory:

I appeal to any white man to say if ever he entered Logan's cabin hungry and he gave him not meat: if ever he came cold and naked and he clothed him not. During the course of the last long and bloody war, Logan remained idle in his cabin, an advocate for peace. Such was my love for the whites that my countrymen pointed as they passed and said, "Logan is the friend of the white men." I had even thought to have lived with you but for the injuries of one man. Colonel Cresap, the last spring, in cold blood and unprovoked, murdered all the relations of Logan, not even sparing my women and children. There remains not a drop of my blood in the veins of any living creature. This called on me for revenge. I have sought it; I have killed many; I have fully glutted my vengeance: for my country I rejoice at the beams of peace. But do not harbor a thought that mine is the joy of fear. Logan never felt fear. He will not turn on his heel to save his life. Who is there to mourn for Logan? Not one.[1]

By rivers and trails, in large and small companies, started home the army that had won the land. The West Fincastle troops, from the lower settlements of the Clinch and Holston valleys, were to return by the Kentucky River, while those from

[1] Some writers have questioned the authenticity of Logan's speech, inclining to think that Gibson himself composed it, partly because of the biblical suggestion in the first few lines. That Gibson gave biblical phraseology to these lines is apparent, though, as Adair points out there are many examples of similitude in Indian and biblical expression. But the thought is Indian and relates to the first article of the Indian's creed, namely, to share his food with the needy. "There remains not a drop of my blood in the veins of any living creature" is a truly Indian lament. Evidently the final four lines of the speech are the most literally translated, for they have the form and the primitive rhythmic beat which a student of Indian poetry quickly recognizes. The authenticity of the speech, as well as the innocence of Cresap, whom Logan mistakenly accused, was vouched for by George Rogers Clark in a letter to Dr. Samuel Brown dated June 17, 1798. See Jefferson papers, Series 5, quoted by English, *Conquest of the Country Northwest of the River Ohio*, vol. ii, p. 1029.

the upper valley would take the shorter way up Sandy Creek. To keep them in provisions during the journey it was ordered that hunters be sent out along these routes to kill and barbecue meat and place it on scaffolds at appropriate spots.

The way home by the Kentucky was a long road for weary and wounded men with hunger gnawing under their belts. We know who swung out along the trail to provide for that little band, "dressed in deerskins colored black, and his hair plaited and bobbed up." It was Daniel Boone — now, by popular demand, Captain Boone — just "discharged from Service," since the valley forts needed him no longer. Once more only a hunter, he went his way over Walden Mountain — past his son's grave marking the place where *he* had been turned back — to serve the men who had opened the gates.

CHAPTER VII

THE DARK AND BLOODY GROUND

WITH the coming of spring Daniel Boone's desire, so long cherished and deferred, to make a way for his neighbors through the wilderness was to be fulfilled at last. But ere his ax could slash the thickets from the homeseekers' path, more than two hundred settlers had entered Kentucky by the northern waterways. Eighty or more of these settled at Harrodsburg, where Harrod was laying out his town on a generous plan, with "in-lots" of half an acre and "out-lots" of larger size. Among those associated with Harrod was George Rogers Clark, who had surveyed claims for himself during the year before the war.

While over two hundred colonists were picking out home sites wherever their pleasure or prudence dictated, a gigantic land promotion scheme — involving the very tracts where they were sowing their first corn — was being set afoot in North

o
129

Carolina by a body of men who figure in the early history of Kentucky as the Transylvania Company. The leader of this organization was Judge Richard Henderson.[1] Judge Henderson dreamed a big dream. His castle in the air had imperial proportions. He resolved, in short, to purchase from the Cherokee Indians the larger part of Kentucky and to establish there a colony after the manner and the economic form of the English Lords Proprietors, whose day in America was so nearly done. Though in the light of history the plan loses none of its dramatic features, it shows the practical defects that must surely have prevented its realization. Like many another Cæsar hungering for empire and staking all to win it, the prospective lord of Kentucky, as we shall see, had left the human equation out of his calculations.

[1] Richard Henderson (1734–1785) was the son of the High Sheriff of Granville County. At first an assistant to his father, he studied law and soon achieved a reputation by the brilliance of his mind and the magnetism of his personality. As presiding Judge at Hillsborough he had come into conflict with the violent element among the Regulators, who had driven him from the court and burned his house and barns. For some time prior to his elevation to the bench, he had been engaged in land speculations. One of Boone's biographers suggests that Boone may have been secretly acting as Henderson's agent during his first lonely explorations of Kentucky. However this may be, it does not appear that Boone and his Yadkin neighbors were acting with Henderson when in September, 1773, they made their first attempt to enter Kentucky as settlers.

Richard Henderson had known Daniel Boone on the Yadkin; and it was Boone's detailed reports of the marvelous richness and beauty of Kentucky which had inspired him to formulate his gigantic scheme and had enabled him also to win to his support several men of prominence in the Back Country. To sound the Cherokees regarding the purchase and to arrange, if possible, for a conference, Henderson dispatched Boone to the Indian towns in the early days of 1775.

Since we have just learned that Dunmore's War compelled the Shawanoes and their allies to relinquish their right to Kentucky, that, both before and after that event, government surveyors were in the territory surveying for the soldiers' claims, and that private individuals had already laid out town sites and staked holdings, it may be asked what right of ownership the Cherokees possessed in Kentucky, that Henderson desired to purchase it of them. The Indian title to Kentucky seems to have been hardly less vague to the red men than it was to the whites. Several of the nations had laid claim to the territory. As late as 1753, it will be remembered, the Shawanoes had occupied a town at Blue Licks, for John Findlay had been taken there by some of them. But, before Findlay

guided Boone through the Gap in 1769, the Shawanoes had been driven out by the Iroquois, who
claimed suzerainty over them as well as over the
Cherokees. In 1768, the Iroquois had ceded Kentucky to the British Crown by the treaty of Fort
Stanwix; whereupon the Cherokees had protested
so vociferously that the Crown's Indian agent, to
quiet them, had signed a collateral agreement with
them. Though claimed by many, Kentucky was
by common consent not inhabited by any of the
tribes. It was the great Middle Ground where the
Indians hunted. It was the Warriors' Path over
which they rode from north and south to slaughter
and where many of their fiercest encounters took
place. However shadowy the title which Henderson purposed to buy, there was one all-sufficing
reason why he must come to terms with the Cherokees: their northernmost towns in Tennessee lay
only fifty or sixty miles below Cumberland Gap and
hence commanded the route over which he must
lead colonists into his empire beyond the hills.

The conference took place early in March, 1775,
at the Sycamore Shoals of the Watauga River.
Twelve hundred Indians, led by their "town
chiefs" — among whom were the old warrior and
the old statesman of their nation, Oconostota and

Attakullakulla — came to the treaty grounds and were received by Henderson and his associates and several hundred white men who were eager for a chance to settle on new lands. Though Boone was now on his way into Kentucky for the Transylvania Company, other border leaders of renown or with their fame still to win were present, and among them James Robertson, of serious mien, and that blond gay knight in buckskin, John Sevier.

It is a dramatic picture we evolve for ourselves from the meager narratives of this event — a mass of painted Indians moving through the sycamores by the bright water, to come presently into a tense, immobile semicircle before the large group of armed frontiersmen seated or standing about Richard Henderson, the man with the imperial dream, the ready speaker whose flashing eyes and glowing oratory won the hearts of all who came under their sway. What though the Cherokee title be a flimsy one at best and the price offered for it a bagatelle! The spirit of Forward March! is there in that great canvas framed by forest and sky. The somber note that tones its lustrous color, as by a sweep of the brush, is the figure of the Chickamaugan chief, Dragging Canoe, warrior and seer and hater of white men, who urges his tribesmen against the sale and, when they will not hearken, springs from their midst into the clear space before Henderson and his band of pioneers and, pointing with uplifted arm, warns them that a dark cloud hangs over the land the white man covets which to the red man has long been a bloody ground.[1]

The purchase, finally consummated, included the country lying between the Kentucky and Cumberland Rivers — almost all the present State of Kentucky, with the adjacent land watered by the Cumberland River and its tributaries, except certain lands previously leased by the Indians to the Watauga Colony. The tract comprised about twenty million acres and extended into Tennessee.

Daniel Boone's work was to cut out a road for the wagons of the Transylvania Company's colonists to pass over. This was to be done by slashing away the briers and underbrush hedging the narrow Warriors' Path that made a direct northward line from Cumberland Gap to the Ohio bank, opposite the mouth of the Scioto River. Just prior to the conference Boone and "thirty guns" had set forth from the Holston to prepare the road and to build a fort on whatever site he should select.

[1] This utterance of Dragging Canoe's is generally supposed to be the origin of the descriptive phrase applied to Kentucky — "the Dark and Bloody Ground." See Roosevelt, *The Winning of the West*, vol. I, p. 229.

By April, Henderson and his first group of tenants were on the trail. In Powell's Valley they came up with a party of Virginians Kentucky bound, led by Benjamin Logan; and the two bands joined together for the march. They had not gone far when they heard disquieting news. After leaving Martin's Station, at the gates of his new domain, Henderson received a letter from Boone telling of an attack by Indians, in which two of his men had been killed, but "we stood on the ground and guarded our baggage till the day and lost nothing."[1] These tidings, indicating that despite treaties and sales, the savages were again on the warpath, might well alarm Henderson's colonists. While they halted, some indecisive, others frankly for retreat, there appeared a company of men making all haste out of Kentucky because of Indian unrest. Six of these Henderson persuaded to turn again and go in with him; but this addition hardly offset the loss of those members of his party who thought it too perilous to proceed. Henderson's own courage did not falter. He had staked his all on this stupendous venture and for him it was forward to wealth and glory or retreat into poverty and eclipse. Boone, in the heart of the danger,

[1] Bogart, *Daniel Boone and the Hunters of Kentucky*, p. 121.

was making the same stand. "If we give way to them [the Indians] now," he wrote, "it will ever be the case."

Signs of discord other than Indian opposition met Henderson as he resolutely pushed on. His conversations with some of the fugitives from Kentucky disclosed the first indications of the storm that was to blow away the empire he was going in to found. He told them that the claims they had staked in Kentucky would not hold good with the Transylvania Company. Whereupon James Mc-Afee, who was leading a group of returning men, stated his opinion that the Transylvania Company's claim would not hold good with Virginia. After the parley, three of McAfee's brothers turned back and went with Henderson's party, but whether with intent to join his colony or to make good their own claims is not apparent. Benjamin Logan continued amicably with Henderson on the march but did not recognize him as Lord Proprietor of Kentucky. He left the Transylvania caravan shortly after entering the territory, branched off in the direction of Harrodsburg, and founded St. Asaph's Station, in the present Lincoln County, independently of Henderson though the site lay within Henderson's purchase.

Notwithstanding delays and apprehensions, Henderson and his colonists finally reached Boone's Fort, which Daniel and his "thirty guns" — lacking two since the Indian encounter — had erected at the mouth of Otter Creek.

An attractive buoyancy of temperament is revealed in Henderson's description in his journal of a giant elm with tall straight trunk and even foliage that shaded a space of one hundred feet. Instantly he chose this "divine elm" as the council chamber of Transylvania. Under its leafage he read the constitution of the new colony. It would be too great a stretch of fancy to call it a democratic document, for it was not that, except in deft phrases. Power was certainly declared to be vested in the people; but the substance of power remained in the hands of the Proprietors.

Terms for land grants were generous enough in the beginning, although Henderson made the fatal mistake of demanding quitrents — one of the causes of dissatisfaction which had led to the Regulators' rising in North Carolina. In September he augmented this error by more than doubling the price of land, adding a fee of eight shillings for surveying, and reserving to the Proprietors one-half of all gold, silver, lead, and sulphur found on

the land. No land near sulphur springs or showing evidences of metals was to be granted to settlers. Moreover, at the Company's store the prices
charged for lead were said to be too high — lead
being necessary for hunting, and hunting being the
only means of procuring food — while the wages
of labor, as fixed by the Company, were too low.
These terms bore too heavily on poor men who
were risking their lives in the colony.

Hence newcomers passed by Boonesborough, as
the Transylvania settlement was presently called,
and went elsewhere. They settled on Henderson's
land but refused his terms. They joined in their
sympathies with James Harrod, who, having established Harrodsburg in the previous year at the
invitation of Virginia, was not in the humor to
acknowledge Henderson's claim or to pay him
tribute. All were willing to combine with the
Transylvania Company for defense, and to enforce
law they would unite in bonds of brotherhood in
Kentucky, even as they had been one with each
other on the earlier frontier now left behind them.
But they would call no man master; they had done
with feudalism. That Henderson should not have
foreseen this, especially after the upheaval in North
Carolina, proves him, in spite of all his brilliant

gifts, to have been a man out of touch with the spirit of the time.

The war of the Revolution broke forth and the Indians descended upon the Kentucky stations. Defense was the one problem in all minds, and defense required powder and lead in plenty. The Transylvania Company was not able to provide the means of defense against the hordes of savages whom Henry Hamilton, the British Governor at Detroit, was sending to make war on the frontiers. Practical men like Harrod and George Rogers Clark — who, if not a practical man in his own interests, was a most practical soldier — saw that unification of interests within the territory with the backing of either Virginia or Congress was necessary. Clark personally would have preferred to see the settlers combine as a freemen's state. It was plain that they would not combine and stake their lives as a unit to hold Kentucky for the benefit of the Transylvania Company, whose authority some of the most prominent men in the territory had refused to recognize. The Proprietary of Transylvania could continue to exist only to the danger of every life in Kentucky.

While the Proprietors sent a delegate to the Continental Congress to win official recognition for

Transylvania, eighty-four men at Harrodsburg drew up a petition addressed to Virginia stating their doubts of the legality of Henderson's title and requesting Virginia to assert her authority according to the stipulations of her charter. That defense was the primary and essential motive of the Harrodsburg Remonstrance seems plain, for when George Rogers Clark set off on foot with one companion to lay the document before the Virginian authorities, he also went to plead for a load of powder. In his account of that hazardous journey, as a matter of fact, he makes scant reference to Transylvania, except to say that the greed of the Proprietors would soon bring the colony to its end, but shows that his mind was seldom off the powder. It is a detail of history that the Continental Congress refused to seat the delegate from Transylvania. Henderson himself went to Virginia to make the fight for his land before the Assembly.[1]

The magnetic center of Boonesborough's life was the lovable and unassuming Daniel Boone. Soon after the building of the fort Daniel had brought in his wife and family. He used often to

[1] In 1778 Virginia disallowed Henderson's title but granted him two hundred thousand acres between the Green and Kentucky rivers for his trouble and expense in opening up the country.

state with a mild pride that his wife and daughters were the first white women to stand on the banks of the Kentucky River. That pride had not been unmixed with anxiety; his daughter Jemima and two daughters of his friend, Richard Calloway, while boating on the river had been captured by Shawanoes and carried off. Boone, accompanied by the girls' lovers and by John Floyd (eager to repay his debt of life-saving to Boone) had pursued them, tracing the way the captors had taken by broken twigs and scraps of dress goods which one of the girls had contrived to leave in their path, had come on the Indians unawares, killed them, and recovered the three girls unhurt.

In the summer of 1776, Virginia took official note of "Captain Boone of Boonesborough," for she sent him a small supply of powder. The men of the little colony, which had begun so pretentiously with its constitution and assembly, were now obliged to put all other plans aside and to concentrate on the question of food and defense. There was a dangerous scarcity of powder and lead. The nearest points at which these necessaries could be procured were the Watauga and Holston River settlements, which were themselves none too well stocked. Harrod and Logan, some time in 1777, reached the Watauga fort with three or four pack-horses and filled their packs from Sevier's store; but, as they neared home, they were detected by red scouts and Logan was badly wounded before he and Harrod were able to drive their precious load safely through the gates at Harrodsburg. In the autumn of 1777, Clark, with a boatload of ammunition, reached Maysville on the Ohio, having successfully run the gauntlet between banks in possession of the foe. He had wrested the powder and lead from the Virginia Council by threats to the effect that if Virginia was so willing to lose Kentucky — for of course "a country not worth defending is not worth claiming" — he and his fellows were quite ready to take Kentucky for themselves and to hold it with their swords against all comers, Virginia included. By even such cogent reasoning had he convinced the Council — which had tried to hedge by expressing doubts that Virginia would receive the Kentucky settlers as "citizens of the State" — that it would be cheaper to give him the powder.

Because so many settlers had fled and the others had come closer together for their common good, Harrodsburg and Boonesborough were now the only occupied posts in Kentucky. Other settlements, once thriving, were abandoned; and, under the terror, the Wild reclaimed them. In April, 1777, Boonesborough underwent its first siege. Boone, leading a sortie, was shot and he fell with a shattered ankle. An Indian rushed upon him and was swinging the tomahawk over him when Simon Kenton, giant frontiersman and hero of many daring deeds, rushed forward, shot the Indian, threw Boone across his back, and fought his way desperately to safety. It was some months ere Boone was his nimble self again. But though he could not "stand up to the guns," he directed all operations from his cabin.

The next year Boone was ready for new ventures growing from the settlers' needs. Salt was necessary to preserve meat through the summer. Accordingly Boone and twenty-seven men went up to the Blue Licks in February, 1778, to replenish their supply by the simple process of boiling the salt water of the Licks till the saline particles adhered to the kettles. Boone was returning alone, with a pack-horse load of salt and game, when a blinding snowstorm overtook him and hid from view four stealthy Shawanoes on his trail. He was seized and carried to a camp of 120 warriors led by the French Canadian, Dequindre, and James and George Girty, two white renegades. Among the

Indians were some of those who had captured him on his first exploring trip through Kentucky and whom he had twice given the slip. Their hilarity was unbounded. Boone quickly learned that this band was on its way to surprise Boonesborough. It was a season when Indian attacks were not expected; nearly threescore of the men were at the salt spring and, to make matters worse, the walls of the new fort where the settlers and their families had gathered were as yet completed on only three sides. Boonesborough was, in short, well-nigh defenseless. To turn the Indians from their purpose, Boone conceived the desperate scheme of offering to lead them to the salt makers' camp with the assurance that he and his companions were willing to join the tribe. He understood Indians well enough to feel sure that once possessed of nearly thirty prisoners, the Shawanoes would not trouble further about Boonesborough but would hasten to make a triumphal entry into their own towns. That some, perhaps all, of the white men would assuredly die, he knew well; but it was the only way to save the women and children in Boonesborough. In spite of Dequindre and the Girtys, who were leading a military expedition for the reduction of a fort, the Shawanoes fell in with the suggestion. When they had taken their prisoners, the more bloodthirsty warriors in the band wanted to tomahawk them all on the spot. By his diplomatic discourse, however, Boone dissuaded them, for the time being at least, and the whole company set off for the towns on the Little Miami.

The weather became severe, very little game crossed their route, and for days they subsisted on slippery elm bark. The lovers of blood did not hold back their scalping knives and several of the prisoners perished; but Black Fish, the chief then of most power in Shawanoe councils, adopted Boone as his son, and gave him the name of Sheltowee, or Big Turtle. Though watched zealously to prevent escape, Big Turtle was treated with every consideration and honor; and, as we would say today, he played the game. He entered into the Indian life with apparent zest, took part in hunts and sports and the races and shooting matches in which the Indians delighted, but he was always careful not to outrun or outshoot his opponents. Black Fish took him to Detroit when some of the tribe escorted the remainder of the prisoners to the British post. There he met Governor Hamilton and, in the hope of obtaining his liberty, he led that dignitary to believe that he and the other people of Boonesborough were eager to move to Detroit and take refuge under the British flag.[1] It is said that Boone always carried in a wallet round his neck the King's commission given him in Dunmore's War; and that he exhibited it to Hamilton to bear out his story. Hamilton sought to ransom him from the Indians, but Black Fish would not surrender his new son. The Governor gave Boone a pony, with saddle and trappings, and other presents, including trinkets to be used in procuring his needs and possibly his liberty from the Shawanoes.

Black Fish then took his son home to Chillicothe. Here Boone found Delawares and Mingos assembling with the main body of the Shawanoe warriors. The war belt was being carried through the Ohio country. Again Boonesborough and Harrodsburg were to be the first settlements attacked. To escape and give warning was now the one purpose that obsessed Boone. He redoubled his efforts to

[1] So well did Boone play his part that he aroused suspicion even in those who knew him best. After his return to Boonesborough his old friend, Calloway, formally accused him of treachery on two counts: that Boone had betrayed the salt makers to the Indians and had planned to betray Boonesborough to the British. Boone was tried and acquitted. His simple explanation of his acts satisfied the court-martial and made him a greater hero than ever among the frontier folk.

throw the Indians off their guard. He sang and whistled blithely about the camp at the mouth of the Scioto River, whither he had accompanied his Indian father to help in the salt boiling. In short, he seemed so very happy that one day Black Fish took his eye off him for a few moments to watch the passing of a flock of turkeys. Big Turtle passed with the flock, leaving no trace. To his lamenting parent it must have seemed as though he had vanished into the air. Daniel crossed the Ohio and ran the 160 miles to Boonesborough in four days, during which time he had only one meal, from a buffalo he shot at the Blue Licks. When he reached the fort after an absence of nearly five months, he found that his wife had given him up for dead and had returned to the Yadkin.

Boone now began with all speed to direct preparations to withstand a siege. Owing to the Indian's leisurely system of councils and ceremonies before taking the warpath, it was not until the first week in September that Black Fish's painted warriors, with some Frenchmen under Dequindre, appeared before Boonesborough. Nine days the siege lasted and was the longest in border history. Dequindre, seeing that the fort might not be taken, resorted to trickery. He requested Boone and a few of his men to come out for a parley, saying that his orders from Hamilton were to protect the lives of the Americans as far as possible. Boone's friend, Calloway, urged against acceptance of the apparently benign proposal which was made, so Dequindre averred, for "bienfaisance et humanité." But the words were the words of a white man, and Boone hearkened to them. With eight of the garrison he went out to the parley. After a long talk in which good will was expressed on both sides, it was suggested by Black Fish that they all shake hands and, as there were so many more Indians than white men, two Indians should, of course, shake hands with one white man, each grasping one of his hands. The moment that their hands gripped, the trick was clear, for the Indians exerted their strength to drag off the white men. Desperate scuffling ensued in which the whites with difficulty freed themselves and ran for the fort. Calloway had prepared for emergencies. The pursuing Indians were met with a deadly fire. After a defeated attempt to mine the fort the enemy withdrew.

The successful defense of Boonesborough was an achievement of national importance, for had Boonesborough fallen, Harrodsburg alone could not have stood. The Indians under the British would have overrun Kentucky; and George Rogers Clark — whose base for his Illinois operations was the Kentucky forts — could not have made the campaigns which wrested the Northwest from the control of Great Britain.

Again Virginia took official note of Captain Boone when in 1779 the Legislature established Boonesborough "a town for the reception of traders" and appointed Boone himself one of the trustees to attend to the sale and registration of lots. An odd office that was for Daniel, who never learned to attend to the registration of his own; he declined it. His name appears again, however, a little later when Virginia made the whole of Kentucky one of her counties with the following officers: Colonel David Robinson, County Lieutenant; George Rogers Clark, Anthony Bledsoe, and John Bowman, Majors; Daniel Boone, James Harrod, Benjamin Logan, and John Todd, Captains.

Boonesborough's successful resistance caused land speculators as well as prospective settlers to take heart of grace. Parties made their way to Boonesborough, Harrodsburg, and even to the Falls of the Ohio, where Clark's fort and blockhouses now stood. In the summer of 1779 Clark had erected on the Kentucky side of the river a large fort which became the nucleus of the town of Louisville. Here, while he was eating his heart out with impatience for money and men to enable him to march to the attack of Detroit, as he had planned, he amused himself by drawing up plans for a city. He laid out private sections and public parks and contemplated the bringing in of families only to inhabit his city, for, oddly enough, he who never married was going to make short shift of mere bachelors in his City Beautiful. Between pen scratches, no doubt, he looked out frequently upon the river to descry if possible a boatload of ammunition or the banners of the troops he had been promised.

When neither appeared, he gave up the idea of Detroit and set about erecting defenses on the southern border, for the Choctaws and Cherokees, united under a white leader named Colbert, were threatening Kentucky by way of the Mississippi. He built in 1780 Fort Jefferson in what is now Ballard County, and had barely completed the new post and garrisoned it with about thirty men when it was besieged by Colbert and his savages. The Indians, assaulting by night, were lured into a position directly before a cannon which poured lead into a mass of them. The remainder fled in terror from the vicinity of the fort; but Colbert succeeded in rallying them and was returning to the attack when he suddenly encountered Clark with a company of men and was forced to abandon his enterprise.

Clark knew that the Ohio Indians would come down on the settlements again during the summer and that to meet their onslaughts every man in Kentucky would be required. He learned that there was a new influx of land seekers over the Wilderness Road and that speculators were doing a thriving business in Harrodsburg; so, leaving his company to protect Fort Jefferson, he took two men with him and started across the wilds on foot for Harrodsburg. To evade the notice of the Indian bands which were moving about the country the three stripped and painted themselves as warriors and donned the feathered headdress. So successful was their disguise that they were fired on by a party of surveyors near the outskirts of Harrodsburg.

The records do not state what were the sensations of certain speculators in a land office in Harrodsburg when a blue-eyed savage in a war

bonnet sprang through the doorway and, with uplifted weapon, declared the office closed; but we
get a hint of the power of Clark's personality and
of his genius for dominating men from the terse
report that he "enrolled" the speculators. He was
informed that another party of men, more nervous
than these, was now on its way out of Kentucky.
In haste he dispatched a dozen frontiersmen to
cut the party off at Crab Orchard and take away
the gun of every man who refused to turn back
and do his bit for Kentucky. To Clark a man
was a gun, and he meant that every gun should
do its duty.

The leaders and pioneers of the Dark and Bloody
Ground were now warriors, all under Clark's command, while for two years longer the Red Terror
ranged Kentucky, falling with savage force now
here, now there. In the first battle of 1780, at the
Blue Licks, Daniel's brother, Edward Boone, was
killed and scalped. Later on in the war his second
son, Israel, suffered a like fate. The toll of life
among the settlers was heavy. Many of the best-
known border leaders were slain. Food and powder often ran short. Corn might be planted, but
whether it would be harvested or not the planters
never knew; and the hunter's rifle shot, necessary

though it was, proved only too often an invitation to the lurking foe. But sometimes, through all the dangers of forest and trail, Daniel Boone slipped away silently to Harrodsburg to confer with Clark; or Clark himself, in the Indian guise that suited the wild man in him not ill, made his way to and from the garrisons which looked to him for everything.

Twice Clark gathered together the "guns" of Kentucky and, marching north into the enemy's country, swept down upon the Indian towns of Piqua and Chillicothe and razed them. In 1782, in the second of these enterprises, his cousin, Joseph Rogers, who had been taken prisoner and adopted by the Indians and then wore Indian garb, was shot down by one of Clark's men. On this expedition Boone and Harrod are said to have accompanied Clark.

The ever present terror and horror of those days, especially of the two years preceding this expedition, are vividly suggested by the quaint remark of an old woman who had lived through them, as recorded for us by a traveler. The most beautiful sight she had seen in Kentucky, she said, was a young man dying a natural death in his bed. Dead but unmarred by hatchet or scalping knife, he was

so rare and comely a picture that the women of the
post sat up all night looking at him.

But, we ask, what golden emoluments were show-
ered by a grateful country on the men who thus
held the land through those years of want and
war, and saved an empire for the Union? What
practical recognition was there of these brave
and unselfish men who daily risked their lives and
faced the stealth and cruelty lurking in the wilderness ways? There is meager eloquence in the records. Here, for instance, is a letter from George
Rogers Clark to the Governor of Virginia, dated
May 27, 1783:

Sir. Nothing but necessity could induce me to make
the following request to Your Excellency, which is to
grant me a small sum of money on account; as I can
assure you, Sir, that I am exceedingly distressed for the
want of necessary clothing etc and don't know any
channel through which I could procure any except of
the Executive. The State I believe will fall consider-
ably in my debt. Any supplies which Your Excellency
favors me with might be deducted out of my accounts.[1]

Clark had spent all his own substance and all else
he could beg, borrow — or appropriate — in the
conquest of Illinois and the defense of Kentucky.

[1] *Calendar of Virginia State Papers*, vol. III, p. 487.

His only reward from Virginia was a grant of land from which he realized nothing, and dismissal from her service when she needed him no longer.

All that Clark had asked for himself was a commission in the Continental Army. This was denied him, as it appears now, not through his own errors, which had not at that time taken hold on him, but through the influence of powerful enemies. It is said that both Spain and England, seeing a great soldier without service for his sword, made him offers, which he refused. As long as any acreage remained to him on which to raise money, he continued to pay the debts he had contracted to finance his expeditions, and in this course he had the assistance of his youngest brother, William, to whom he assigned his Indiana grant.

His health impaired by hardship and exposure and his heart broken by his country's indifference, Clark sank into alcoholic excesses. In his sixtieth year, just six years before his death, and when he was a helpless paralytic, he was granted a pension of four hundred dollars. There is a ring of bitter irony in the words with which he accepted the sword sent him by Virginia in his crippled old age: "When Virginia needed a sword I gave her one." He died near Louisville on February 13, 1818.

Kentucky was admitted to the Union in 1792. But even before Kentucky became a State her affairs, particularly as to land, were arranged, let us say, on a practical business basis. Then it was discovered that Daniel Boone had no legal claim to any foot of ground in Kentucky. Daniel owned nothing but the clothes he wore; and for those — as well as for much powder, lead, food, and such trifles — he was heavily in debt.

So, in 1788, Daniel Boone put the list of his debts in his wallet, gathered his wife and his younger sons about him, and, shouldering his hunter's rifle, once more turned towards the wilds. The country of the Great Kanawha in West Virginia was still a wilderness, and a hunter and trapper might, in some years, earn enough to pay his debts. For others, now, the paths he had hewn and made safe; for Boone once more the wilderness road.

CHAPTER VIII

TENNESSEE

Indian law, tradition, and even superstition had shaped the conditions which the pioneers faced when they crossed the mountains. This savage inheritance had decreed that Kentucky should be a dark and bloody ground, fostering no life but that of four-footed beasts, its fertile sod never to stir with the green push of the corn. And so the white men who went into Kentucky to build and to plant went as warriors go, and for every cabin they erected they battled as warriors to hold a fort. In the first years they planted little corn and reaped less, for it may be said that their rifles were never out of their hands. We have seen how stations were built and abandoned until but two stood. Untiring vigilance and ceaseless warfare were the price paid by the first Kentuckians ere they turned the Indian's place of desolation and death into a land productive and a living habitation.

157

Herein lies the difference, slight apparently, yet significant, between the first Kentucky and the first Tennessee[1] colonies. Within the memory of the Indians only one tribe had ever attempted to make their home in Kentucky — a tribe of the fighting Shawanoes — and they had been terribly chastised for their temerity. But Tennessee was the home of the Cherokees, and at Chickasaw Bluffs (Memphis) began the southward trail to the principal towns of the Chickasaws. By the red man's fiat, then, human life might abide in Tennessee, though not in Kentucky, and it followed that in seasons of peace the frontiersmen might settle in Tennessee. So it was that as early as 1757, before the great Cherokee war, a company of Virginians under Andrew Lewis had, on an invitation from the Indians, erected Fort Loudon near Great Telliko, the Cherokees' principal town, and that, after the treaty of peace in 1761, Waddell and his rangers of North Carolina had erected a fort on the Holston.

Though Fort Loudon had fallen tragically during the war, and though Waddell's fort had been

[1] Tennessee. The name, Ten-as-se, appears on Adair's map as one of the old Cherokee towns. Apparently neither the meaning nor the reason why the colonists called both state and river by this name has been handed down to us.

abandoned, neither was without influence in the colonization of Tennessee, for some of the men who built these forts drifted back a year or two later and set up the first cabins on the Holston. These earliest settlements, thin and scattered, did not survive; but in 1768 the same settlers or others of their kind — discharged militiamen from Back Country regiments — once more made homes on the Holston. They were joined by a few families from near the present Raleigh, North Carolina, who had despaired of seeing justice done to the tenants on the mismanaged estates of Lord Granville. About the same time there was erected the first cabin on the Watauga River, as is generally believed, by a man of the name of William Bean (or Been), hunter and frontier soldier from Pittsylvania County, Virginia. This man, who had hunted on the Watauga with Daniel Boone in 1760, chose as the site of his dwelling the place of the old hunting camp near the mouth of Boone's Creek. He soon began to have neighbors.

Meanwhile the Regulation Movement stirred the Back Country of both the Carolinas. In 1768, the year in which William Bean built his cabin on the bank of the Watauga, five hundred armed

Regulators in North Carolina, aroused by irregularities in the conduct of public office, gathered to assert their displeasure, but dispersed peaceably on receipt of word from Governor Tryon that he had ordered the prosecution of any officer found guilty of extortion. Edmund Fanning, the most hated of Lord Granville's agents, though convicted, escaped punishment. Enraged at this miscarriage of justice, the Regulators began a system of terrorization by taking possession of the court, presided over by Richard Henderson. The judge himself was obliged to slip out by a back way to avoid personal injury. The Regulators burned his house and stable. They meted out mob treatment likewise to William Hooper, later one of the signers of the Declaration of Independence.

Two elements, with antithetical aims, had been at work in the Regulation; and the unfortunate failure of justice in the case of Fanning had given the corrupt element its opportunity to seize control. In the petitions addressed to Governor Tryon by the leaders of the movement in its earlier stages the aims of liberty-loving thinkers are traceable. It is worthy of note that they included in their demands articles which are now constitutional. They desired that "suffrage be given by ticket and ballot"; that the mode of taxation be altered, and each person be taxed in proportion to the profits arising from his estate; that judges and clerks be given salaries instead of perquisites and fees. They likewise petitioned for repeal of the act prohibiting dissenting ministers from celebrating the rites of matrimony. The establishment of these reforms, the petitioners of the Regulation concluded, would "conciliate" their minds to "every just measure of government, and would make the laws what the Constitution ever designed they should be, their protection and not their bane." Herein clearly enough we can discern the thought and the phraseology of the Ulster Presbyterians.

But a change took place in both leaders and methods. During the Regulators' career of violence they were under the sway of an agitator named Hermon Husband. This demagogue was reported to have been expelled from the Quaker Society for cause; it is on record that he was expelled from the North Carolina Assembly because a vicious anonymous letter was traced to him. He deserted his dupes just before the shots cracked at Alamance Creek and fled from the colony. He was afterwards apprehended in Pennsylvania for complicity in the Whisky Insurrection.

Four of the leading Presbyterian ministers of the Back Country issued a letter in condemnation of the Regulators. One of these ministers was the famous David Caldwell, son-in-law of the Reverend Alexander Craighead, and a man who knew the difference between liberty and license and who proved himself the bravest of patriots in the War of Independence. The records of the time contain sworn testimony against the Regulators by Waightstill Avery, a signer of the Mecklenburg Resolves, who later presided honorably over courts in the western circuit of Tennessee; and there is evidence indicating Jacobite and French intrigue. That Governor Tryon recognized a hidden hand at work seems clearly revealed in his proclamation addressed to those "whose understandings have been run away with and whose passions have been led in captivity by some evil designing men who, actuated by cowardice and a sense of that Publick Justice which is due to their Crimes, have obscured themselves from Publick view." What the Assembly thought of the Regulators was expressed in 1770 in a drastic bill which so shocked the authorities in England that instructions were sent forbidding any Governor to approve such a bill in future, declaring it "a disgrace to the British Statute Books."

On May 16, 1771, some two thousand Regulators were precipitated by Husband into the Battle of Alamance, which took place in a district settled largely by a rough and ignorant type of Germans, many of whom Husband had lured to swell his mob. Opposed to him were eleven hundred of Governor Tryon's troops, officered by such patriots as Griffith Rutherford, Hugh Waddell, and Francis Nash. During an hour's engagement about twenty Regulators were killed, while the Governor's troops had nine killed and sixty-one wounded. Six of the leaders were hanged. The rest took the oath of allegiance which Tryon administered.

It has been said about the Regulators that they were not cast down by their defeat at Alamance but "like the mammoth, they shook the bolt from their brow and crossed the mountains," but such flowery phrases do not seem to have been inspired by facts. Nor do the records show that "fifteen hundred Regulators" arrived at Watauga in 1771, as has also been stated. Nor are the names of the leaders of the Regulation to be found in the list of signatures affixed to the one "state paper" of Watauga which was preserved and written into historic annals. Nor yet do those names appear on the roster of the Watauga and Holston men who, in 1774, fought with Shelby under Andrew Lewis in the Battle of Point Pleasant. The Boones and the Bryans, the Robertsons, the Seviers, the Shelbys, the men who opened up the West and shaped the destiny of its inhabitants, were genuine freemen, with a sense of law and order as inseparable from liberty. They would follow a Washington but not a Hermon Husband.

James Hunter, whose signature leads on all Regulation manifestoes just prior to the Battle of Alamance, was a sycophant of Husband, to whom he addressed fulsome letters; and in the real battle for democracy — the War of Independence — he was a Tory. The Colonial Records show that those who, "like the mammoth," shook from them the ethical restraints which make man superior to the giant beast, and who later bolted into the mountains, contributed chiefly the lawlessness that harassed the new settlements. They were the banditti and, in 1776, the Tories of the western hills; they pillaged the homes of the men who were fighting for the democratic ideal.

It was not the Regulation Movement which turned westward the makers of the Old Southwest, but the free and enterprising spirit of the age.

It was emphatically an age of doers; and if men who felt the constructive urge in them might not lay hold on conditions where they were and re-shape them, then they must go forward seeking that environment which would give their genius its opportunity.

Of such adventurous spirits was James Robertson, a Virginian born of Ulster Scot parentage, and a resident of (the present) Wake County, North Carolina, since his boyhood. Robertson was twenty-eight years old when, in 1770, he rode over the hills to Watauga. We can imagine him as he was then, for the portrait taken much later in life shows the type of face that does not change. It is a high type combining the best qualities of his race. Intelligence, strength of purpose, fortitude, and moral power are there; they impress us at the first glance. At twenty-eight he must have been a serious young man, little given to laughter; indeed, spontaneity is perhaps the only good trait we miss in studying his face. He was a thinker who had not yet found his purpose — a thinker in leash, for at this time James Robertson could neither read nor write.

At Watauga, Robertson lived for a while in the cabin of a man named Honeycut. He chose land for himself and, in accordance with the custom of the time, sealed his right to it by planting corn. He remained to harvest his first crop and then set off to gather his family and some of his friends together and escort them to the new country. But on the way he missed the trail and wandered for a fortnight in the mountains. The heavy rains ruined his powder so that he could not hunt; for food he had only berries and nuts. At one place, where steep bluffs opposed him, he was obliged to abandon his horse and scale the mountain side on foot. He was in extremity when he chanced upon two huntsmen who gave him food and set him on the trail. If this experience proves his lack of the hunter's instinct and the woodsman's resourcefulness which Boone possessed, it proves also his special qualities of perseverance and endurance which were to reach their zenith in his successful struggle to colonize and hold western Tennessee. He returned to Watauga in the following spring (1771) with his family and a small group of colonists. Robertson's wife was an educated woman and under her instruction he now began to study.

Next year a young Virginian from the Shenandoah Valley rode on down Holston Valley on a hunting and exploring trip and loitered at Watauga.

Here he found not only a new settlement but an independent government in the making; and forthwith he determined to have a part in both. This young Virginian had already shown the inclination of a political colonist, for in the Shenandoah Valley he had, at the age of nineteen, laid out the town of New Market (which exists to this day) and had directed its municipal affairs and invited and fostered its clergy. This young Virginian — born on September 23, 1745, and so in 1772 twenty-seven years of age — was John Sevier, that John Sevier whose monument now towers from its site in Knoxville to testify of both the wild and the great deeds of old Tennessee's beloved knight. Like Robertson, Sevier hastened home and removed his whole family, including his wife and children, his parents and his brothers and sisters, to this new haven of freedom at Watauga.

The friendship formed between Robertson and Sevier in these first years of their work together was never broken, yet two more opposite types could hardly have been brought together. Robertson was a man of humble origin, unlettered, not a dour Scot but a solemn one. Sevier was cavalier as well as frontiersman. On his father's side he was of the patrician family of Xavier in France. His progenitors, having become Huguenots, had taken refuge in England, where the name Xavier was finally changed to Sevier. John Sevier's mother was an Englishwoman. Some years before his birth his parents had emigrated to the Shenandoah Valley. Thus it happened that John Sevier, who mingled good English blood with the blue blood of old France, was born an American and grew up a frontier hunter and soldier. He stood about five feet nine from his moccasins to his crown of light brown hair. He was well-proportioned and as graceful of body as he was hard-muscled and swift. His chin was firm, his nose of a Roman cast, his mouth well-shaped, its slightly full lips slanting in a smile that would not be repressed. Under the high, finely modeled brow, small keen dark blue eyes sparkled with health, with intelligence, and with the man's joy in life.

John Sevier indeed cannot be listed as a type; he was individual. There is no other character like him in border annals. He was cavalier and prince in his leadership of men; he had their homage. Yet he knew how to be comrade and brother to the lowliest. He won and held the confidence and friendship of the serious-minded Robertson no less than the idolatry of the wildest spirits on the frontier throughout the forty-three years of the spectacular career which began for him on the day he brought his tribe to Watauga. In his time he wore the governor's purple; and a portrait painted of him shows how well this descendant of the noble Xaviers could fit himself to the dignity and formal habiliments of state. Yet in the fringed deerskin of frontier garb, he was fleeter on the warpath than the Indians who fled before him; and he could outride and outshoot — and, it is said, outswear — the best and the worst of the men who followed him. Perhaps the lurking smile on John Sevier's face was a flicker of mirth that there should be found any man, red or white, with temerity enough to try conclusions with him. None ever did, successfully.

The historians of Tennessee state that the Wataugans formed their government in 1772 and that Sevier was one of its five commissioners. Yet, as Sevier did not settle in Tennessee before 1773, it is possible that the Watauga Association was not formed until then. Unhappily the written constitution of the little commonwealth was not preserved; but it is known that, following the Ulsterman's ideal, manhood suffrage and religious independence were two of its provisions. The commissioners enlisted a militia and they recorded deeds for land, issued marriage licenses, and tried offenders against the law. They believed themselves to be within the boundaries of Virginia and therefore adopted the laws of that State for their guidance. They had numerous offenders to deal with, for men fleeing from debt or from the consequence of crime sought the new settlements just across the mountains as a safe and adjacent harbor. The attempt of these men to pursue their lawlessness in Watauga was one reason why the Wataugans organized a government.

When the line was run between Virginia and North Carolina beyond the mountains, Watauga was discovered to be south of Virginia's limits and hence on Indian lands. This was in conflict with the King's Proclamation, and Alexander Cameron, British agent to the Cherokees, accordingly ordered the encroaching settlers to depart. The Indians, however, desired them to remain. But since it was illegal to purchase Indian lands, Robertson negotiated a lease for ten years. In 1775, when Henderson made his purchase from the Cherokees, at Sycamore Shoals on the Watauga, Robertson and Sevier, who were present at the sale with other Watauga commissioners, followed Henderson's example and bought outright the lands they desired to include in Watauga's domain. In 1776 they petitioned North Carolina for "annexation." As they were already within North Carolina's bounds, it was recognition rather than annexation which they sought. This petition, which is the only Wataugan document to survive, is undated but marked as received in August, 1776. It is in Sevier's handwriting and its style suggests that it was composed by him, for in its manner of expression it has much in common with many later papers from his pen. That Wataugans were a law-loving community and had formed their government for the purpose of making law respected is reiterated throughout the document. As showing the quality of these first western statemakers, two paragraphs are quoted:

Finding ourselves on the frontiers, and being apprehensive that for want of proper legislature we might become a shelter for such as endeavored to defraud their creditors; considering also the necessity of recording deeds, wills, and doing other public business; we, by consent of the people, formed a court for the purposes above mentioned, taking, by desire of our constituents, the Virginia laws for our guide, so near as the situation of affairs would permit. This was intended for ourselves, and *was done by consent of every individual*.

The petition goes on to state that, among their measures for upholding law, the Wataugans had enlisted "a company of fine riflemen" and put them under command of "Captain James Robertson."

We . . . thought proper to station them on our frontiers in defense of the common cause, at the expense and risque of our own private fortunes, till farther public orders, which we flatter ourselves will give no offense. . . . We pray your mature and deliberate consideration in our behalf, that you may annex us to your Province (whether as county, district, or other division) in such manner as may enable us to share in the glorious cause of Liberty: enforce our laws under authority and in every respect become the best members of society; and for ourselves and our constituents we hope we may venture to assure you that we shall adhere strictly to your determinations, and that nothing will be lacking or anything neglected that may add weight (in the civil or military establishments) to the glorious cause in which we are now struggling, or contribute to the welfare of our own or ages yet to come.

One hundred and thirteen names are signed to the document. In the following year (1777) North Carolina erected her overhill territory into Washington County. The Governor appointed justices of the peace and militia officers who in the following year organized the new county and its courts. And so Watauga's independent government, begun in the spirit of true liberty, came as lawfully to its end.

But for nearly three years before their political status was thus determined, the Wataugans were sharing "in the glorious cause of Liberty" by defending their settlements against Indian attacks. While the majority of the young Cherokee warriors were among their enemies, their chief battles were fought with those from the Chickamaugan towns on the Tennessee River, under the leadership of Dragging Canoe. The Chickamaugans embraced the more vicious and bloodthirsty Cherokees, with a mixture of Creeks and bad whites, who, driven from every law-abiding community, had cast in their lot with this tribe. The exact number of white thieves and murderers who had found harbor in the Indian towns during a score or more of years is not known; but the letters of the Indian agents, preserved in the records, would indicate that there were a good many of them. They were fit allies for Dragging Canoe; their hatred of those from whom their own degeneracy had separated them was not less than his.

In July, 1776, John Sevier wrote to the Virginia Committee as follows:

DEAR GENTLEMEN: Isaac Thomas, William Falling, Jaret Williams and one more have this moment come in by making their escape from the Indians and say six hundred Indians and whites were to start for this fort and intend to drive the country up to New River before they return.

Thus was heralded the beginning of a savage warfare which kept the borderers engaged for years.

It has been a tradition of the chroniclers that Isaac Thomas received a timely warning from Nancy Ward, a half-caste Cherokee prophetess who often showed her good will towards the whites; and that the Indians were roused to battle by Alexander Cameron and John Stuart, the British agents or superintendents among the overhill tribes. There was a letter bearing Cameron's name stating that fifteen hundred savages from the Cherokee and Creek nations were to join with British troops landed at Pensacola in an expedition against the southern frontier colonies. This letter was brought to Watauga at dead of night by a masked man who slipped it through a window and rode away. Apparently John Sevier did not believe the military information contained in the mysterious missive, for he communicated nothing of it to the Virginia Committee. In recent years the facts have come to light. This mysterious letter and others of a similar tenor bearing forged signatures are cited in a report by the British Agent, John Stuart, to his Government. It appears that such inflammatory missives had been industriously scattered through the back settlements of both Carolinas. There are also letters from Stuart to Lord Dartmouth, dated a year earlier, urging that something be done immediately to counteract rumors set afloat that the British were endeavoring to instigate both the Indians and the negroes to attack the Americans.

Now it is, of course, an established fact that both the British and the American armies used Indians in the War of Independence, even as both together had used them against the French and the Spanish and their allied Indians. It was inevitable that the Indians should participate in any severe conflict between the whites. They were a numerous and a warlike people and, from their point of view, they had more at stake than the alien whites who were contesting for control of the red man's continent. Both British and Americans have been blamed for "half-hearted attempts to keep the Indians neutral." The truth is that each side strove to enlist the Indians — to be used, if needed later, as warriors. Massacre was no part of this policy, though it may have been countenanced by individual officers in both camps. But it is obvious

that, once the Indians took the warpath, they were
to be restrained by no power and, no matter under
whose nominal command, they would carry on
warfare by their own methods.[1]

Whatever may have been the case elsewhere, the
attacks on the Watauga and Holston settlements

[1] "There is little doubt that either side, British or Americans, stood
ready to enlist the Indians. Already before Boston the Americans
had had the help of the Stockbridge tribe. Washington found the
service committed to the practise when he arrived at Cambridge early
in July. Dunmore had taken the initiative in securing such allies, at
least in purpose; but the insurgent Virginians had had of late more
direct contact with the tribes and were now striving to secure them
but with little success." *The Westward Movement*, by Justin Winsor,
p. 87.

General Ethan Allen of Vermont, as his letters show, sent emissaries
into Canada in an endeavor to enlist the French Canadians and the
Canadian Indians against the British in Canada. See *American Archives*, Fourth Series, vol. II, p. 714. The British General Gage wrote
to Lord Dartmouth from Boston, June 12, 1775: "We need not be
tender of calling on the Savages as the rebels have shown us the
example, by bringing as many Indians down against us as they could
collect." *American Archives*, Fourth Series, vol. II, p. 967.

In a letter to Lord Germain, dated August 23, 1776, John Stuart
wrote: "Although Mr. Cameron was in constant danger of assassina-
tion and the Indians were threatened with invasion should they dare
to protect him, yet he still found means to prevent their falling on the
settlement." See North Carolina *Colonial Records*, vol. x, pp. 608
and 763. Proof that the British agents had succeeded in keeping the
Cherokee neutral till the summer of 1776 is found in the instructions,
dated the 7th of July, to Major Winston from President Rutledge of
South Carolina, regarding the Cherokees, that they must be forced to
give up the British agents and "*instead of remaining in a State of
Neutrality* with respect to British Forces they must take part with us
against them." See North Carolina *Colonial Records*, vol. x, p. 658.

were not instigated by British agents. It was not Nancy Ward but Henry Stuart, John Stuart's deputy, who sent Isaac Thomas to warn the settlers. In their efforts to keep the friendship of the red men, the British and the Americans were providing them with powder and lead. The Indians had run short of ammunition and, since hunting was their only means of livelihood, they must shoot or starve. South Carolina sent the Cherokees a large supply of powder and lead which was captured en route by Tories. About the same time Henry Stuart set out from Pensacola with another consignment from the British. His report to Lord Germain of his arrival in the Chickamaugan towns and of what took place there just prior to the raids on the Tennessee settlements is one of the most illuminating as well as one of the most dramatic papers in the collected records of that time.[1]

Stuart's first act was secretly to send out Thomas, the trader, to warn the settlers of their peril, for a small war party of braves was even then concluding the preliminary war ceremonies. The reason for this Indian alarm and projected excursion was the fact that the settlers had built one fort at least on the Indian lands. Stuart finally persuaded the

[1] North Carolina *Colonial Records*, vol. x, pp. 763–785.

12

Indians to remain at peace until he could write to the settlers stating the grievances and asking for negotiations. The letters were to be carried by Thomas on his return.

But no sooner was Thomas on his way again with the letters than there arrived a deputation of warriors from the Northern tribes — from "the Confederate nations, the Mohawks, Ottawas, Nantucas, Shawanoes and Delawares" — fourteen men in all, who entered the council hall of the Old Beloved Town of Chota with their faces painted black and the war belt carried before them. They said that they had been seventy days on their journey. Everywhere along their way they had seen houses and forts springing up like weeds across the green sod of their hunting lands. Where once were great herds of deer and buffalo, they had watched thousands of men at arms preparing for war. So many now were the white warriors and their women and children that the red men had been obliged to travel a great way on the other side of the Ohio and to make a detour of nearly three hundred miles to avoid being seen. Even on this outlying route they had crossed the fresh tracks of a great body of people with horses and cattle going still further towards the setting sun. But their

cries were not to be in vain; for "their fathers, the French" had heard them and had promised to aid them if they would now strike as one for their lands.

After this preamble the deputy of the Mohawks rose. He said that some American people had made war on one of their towns and had seized the son of their Great Beloved Man, Sir William Johnson, imprisoned him, and put him to a cruel death; this crime demanded a great vengeance and they would not cease until they had taken it. One after another the fourteen delegates rose and made their "talks" and presented their wampum strings to Dragging Canoe. The last to speak was a chief of the Shawanoes. He also declared that "their fathers, the French," who had been so long dead, were "alive again," that they had supplied them plentifully with arms and ammunition and had promised to assist them in driving out the Americans and in reclaiming their country. Now all the Northern tribes were joined in one for this great purpose; and they themselves were on their way to all the Southern tribes and had resolved that, if any tribe refused to join, they would fall upon and extirpate that tribe, after having overcome the whites. At the conclusion of his oration the Shawanoe presented the war belt — nine feet of six-inch-wide purple wampum spattered with vermilion — to Dragging Canoe, who held it extended between his two hands, in silence, and waited. Presently rose a headman whose wife had been a member of Sir William Johnson's household. He laid his hand on the belt and sang the war song. One by one, then, chiefs and warriors rose, laid hold of the great belt and chanted the war song. Only the older men, made wise by many defeats, sat still in their places, mute and dejected. "After that day every young fellow's face in the overhills towns appeared blackened and nothing was now talked of but war."

Stuart reports that "all the white men" in the tribe also laid hands on the belt. Dragging Canoe then demanded that Cameron and Stuart come forward and take hold of the war belt — "which we refused." Despite the offense their refusal gave — and it would seem a dangerous time to give such offense — Cameron delivered a "strong talk" for peace, warning the Cherokees of what must surely be the end of the rashness they contemplated. Stuart informed the chief that if the Indians persisted in attacking the settlements without waiting for answers to his letters, he would not remain with them any longer or bring them any more ammunition. He went to his house and

made ready to leave on the following day. Early
the next morning Dragging Canoe appeared at his
door and told him that the Indians were now very
angry about the letters he had written, which could
only have put the settlers on their guard; and that
if any white man attempted to leave the nation
"they had determined to follow him *but not to
bring him back.*" Dragging Canoe had painted his
face black to carry this message. Thomas now
returned with an answer from "the West Fincastle men," which was so unsatisfactory to the
tribe that war ceremonies were immediately begun.
Stuart and Cameron could no longer influence the
Indians. "All that could now be done was to give
them strict charge not to pass the Boundary Line,
not to injure any of the King's faithful subjects, not
to Kill any women and children"; and to threaten
to "stop all ammunition" if they did not obey
these orders.

The major part of the Watauga militia went out
to meet the Indians and defeated a large advance
force at Long Island Flats on the Holston. The
Watauga fort, where many of the settlers had taken
refuge, contained forty fighting men under Robertson and Sevier. As Indians usually retreated and

waited for a while after a defeat, those within the fort took it for granted that no immediate attack was to be expected; and the women went out at daybreak into the fields to milk the cows. Suddenly the war whoop shrilled from the edge of the clearing. Red warriors leaped from the green skirting of the forest. The women ran for the fort. Quickly the heavy gates swung to and the dropped bar secured them. Only then did the watchmen discover that one woman had been shut out. She was a young woman nearing her twenties and, if legend has reported her truly, "Bonnie Kate Sherrill" was a beauty. Through a porthole Sevier saw her running towards the shut gates, dodging and darting, her brown hair blowing from the wind of her race for life — and offering far too rich a prize to the yelling fiends who dashed after her. Sevier coolly shot the foremost of her pursuers, then sprang upon the wall, caught up Bonnie Kate, and tossed her inside to safety. And legend says further that when, after Sevier's brief widowerhood, she became his wife, four years later, Bonnie Kate was wont to say that she would be willing to run another such race any day to have another such introduction!

There were no casualties within the fort and,

after three hours, the foe withdrew, leaving several of their warriors slain.

In the excursions against the Indians which followed this opening of hostilities Sevier won his first fame as an "Indian fighter" — the fame later crystallized in the phrase "thirty-five battles, thirty-five victories." His method was to take a very small company of the hardiest and swiftest horsemen — men who could keep their seat and endurance, and horses that could keep their feet and their speed, on any steep of the mountains no matter how tangled and rough the going might be — swoop down upon war camp, or town, and go through it with rifle and hatchet and fire, then dash homeward at the same pace before the enemy had begun to consider whether to follow him or not. In all his "thirty-five battles" it is said he lost not more than fifty men.

The Cherokees made peace in 1777, after about a year of almost continuous warfare, the treaty being concluded on their side by the old chiefs who had never countenanced the war. Dragging Canoe refused to take part, but he was rendered innocuous for the time being by the destruction of several of the Chickamaugan villages. James Robertson now went to Chota as Indian agent for North Carolina.

So fast was population growing, owing to the opening of a wagon road into Burke County, North Carolina, that Washington County was divided. John Sevier became Colonel of Washington and Isaac Shelby Colonel of the newly erected Sullivan County. Jonesborough, the oldest town in Tennessee, was laid out as the county seat of Washington; and in the same year (1778) Sevier moved to the bank of the Nolichucky River, so-called after the Indian name of this dashing sparkling stream, meaning *rapid* or *precipitous*. Thus the nickname given John Sevier by his devotees had a dual application. He was well called Nolichucky Jack.

When Virginia annulled Richard Henderson's immense purchase but allowed him a large tract on the Cumberland, she by no means discouraged that intrepid pioneer. Henderson's tenure of Kentucky had been brief, but not unprofitable in experience. He had learned that colonies must be treated with less commercial pressure and with more regard to individual liberty, if they were to be held loyal either to a King beyond the water or to an uncrowned leader nearer at hand. He had been making his plans for colonization of that portion of the Transylvania purchase which lay within the bounds of North Carolina along the Cumberland and choosing his men to lay the foundations of his projected settlement in what was then a wholly uninhabited country; and he had decided on generous terms, such as ten dollars a thousand acres for land, the certificate of purchase to entitle the holder to further proceedings in the land office without extra fees.

To head an enterprise of such danger and hardship Henderson required a man of more than mere courage; a man of resource, of stability, of proven powers, one whom other men would follow and obey with confidence. So it was that James Robertson was chosen to lead the first white settlers into middle Tennessee. He set out in February, 1779, accompanied by his brother, Mark Robertson, several other white men, and a negro, to select a site for settlement and to plant corn. Meanwhile another small party led by Gaspar Mansker had arrived. As the boundary line between Virginia and North Carolina had not been run to this point, Robertson believed that the site he had chosen lay within Virginia and was in the disposal of General Clark. To protect the settlers, therefore, he journeyed into the Illinois country to purchase cabin rights from Clark, but there he was evidently convinced that the site on the Cumberland would be found to lie within North Carolina. He returned to Watauga to lead a party of settlers into the new territory, towards which they set out in October. After crossing the mountain chain through Cumberland Gap, the party followed Boone's road — the Warriors' Path — for some distance and then made their own trail southwestward through the wilderness to the bluffs on the Cumberland, where they built cabins to house them against one of the coldest winters ever experienced in that country. So were laid the first foundations of the present city of Nashville, at first named Nashborough by Robertson.[1] On the way, Robertson had fallen in with a party of men and families bound for Kentucky and had persuaded them to accompany his little band to the Cumberland. Robertson's own wife and children, as well as the families of his party, had been left to follow in the second expedition, which was to be made by water under the command of Captain John Donelson.

The little fleet of boats containing the settlers, their families, and all their household goods, was to start from Fort Patrick Henry, near Long Island

[1] In honor of General Francis Nash, of North Carolina, who was mortally wounded at Germantown, 1777.

in the Holston River, to float down into the Tennessee and along the 652 miles of that widely wan-
dering stream to the Ohio, and then to proceed up
the Ohio to the mouth of the Cumberland and up
the Cumberland until Robertson's station should
appear — a journey, as it turned out, of some nine
hundred miles through unknown country and on
waters at any rate for the greater part never before
navigated by white men.

*Journal of a voyage, intended by God's permis-
sion, in the good boat Adventure* is the title of the
log book in which Captain Donelson entered the
events of the four months' journey. Only a few
pages endured to be put into print: but those few
tell a tale of hazard and courage that seems complete. Could a lengthier narrative, even if en-
riched with literary art and fancy, bring before us
more vividly than do the simple entries of Donelson's log the spirit of the men and the women who
won the West? If so little personal detail is recorded of the pioneer men of that day that we must
deduce what they were from what they did, what
do we know of their unfailing comrades, the pioneer women? Only that they were there and that
they shared in every test of courage and endurance, save the march of troops and the hunt.

Donelson's *Journal* therefore has a special value, because in its terse account of Mrs. Jennings and Mrs. Peyton it depicts unforgettably the quality of pioneer womanhood.[1]

December 22nd, 1779. Took our departure from the fort and fell down the river to the mouth of Reedy Creek where we were stopped by the fall of water and most excessive hard frost.

Perhaps part of the *Journal* was lost, or perhaps the "excessive hard frost" of that severe winter, when it is said even droves of wild game perished, prevented the boats from going on, for the next entry is dated the 27th of February. On this date the *Adventure* and two other boats grounded and lay on the shoals all that afternoon and the succeeding night "in much distress."

March 2nd. Rain about half the day. . . . Mr. Henry's boat being driven on the point of an island by the force of the current was sunk, the whole cargo much damaged and the crew's lives much endangered, which occasioned the whole fleet to put on shore and go to their assistance. . . .

Monday 6th. Got under way before sunrise; the morning proving very foggy, many of the fleet were much bogged — about 10 o'clock lay by for them; when

[1] This *Journal* is printed in Ramsey's *Annals of Tennessee.*

collected, proceeded down. Camped on the north shore, where Captain Hutching's negro man died, being much frosted in his feet and legs, of which he died.

Tuesday, 7th. Got under way very early; the day proving very windy, a S. S. W., and the river being wide occasioned a high sea, insomuch that some of the smaller crafts were in danger; therefore came to at the uppermost Chiccamauga town, which was then evacuated, where we lay by that afternoon and camped that night. The wife of Ephraim Peyton was here delivered of a child. Mr. Peyton has gone through by land with Captain Robertson.

Wednesday 8th . . . proceed down to an Indian village which was inhabited . . . they insisted on us to come ashore, called us brothers, and showed other signs of friendship. . . . And here we must regret the unfortunate death of young Mr. Payne, on board Captain Blakemore's boat, who was mortally wounded by reason of the boat running too near the northern shore opposite the town, where some of the enemy lay concealed; and the more tragical misfortune of poor Stuart, his family and friends, to the number of twenty-eight persons. This man had embarked with us for the Western country, but his family being diseased with the small pox, it was agreed upon between him and the company that he should keep at some distance in the rear, for fear of the infection spreading, and he was warned each night when the encampment should take place by the sound of a horn. . . . the Indians having now collected to a considerable number, observing his helpless situation singled off from the rest of the fleet, intercepted him and killed and took prisoners the whole crew . . . ; their cries were distinctly heard. . . .

After describing a running fight with Indians stationed on the bluffs on both shores where the river narrowed to half its width and boiled through a canyon, the entry for the day concludes: "Jennings's boat is missing."

Friday 10th. This morning about 4 o'clock we were surprised by the cries of "help poor Jennings" at some distance in the rear. He had discovered us by our fires and came up in the most wretched condition. He states that as soon as the Indians discovered his situation [his boat had run on a rock] they turned their whole attention to him and kept up a most galling fire at his boat. He ordered his wife, a son nearly grown, a young man who accompanies them and his negro man and woman, to throw all his goods into the river to lighten their boat for the purpose of getting her off; himself returning their fire as well as he could, being a good soldier and an excellent marksman. But before they had accomplished their object, his son, the young man and the negro, jumped out of the boat and left. . . . Mrs. Jennings, however, and the negro woman, succeeded in unloading the boat, but chiefly by the exertions of Mrs. Jennings who got out of the boat and shoved her off, but was near falling a victim to her own intrepidity on account of the boat starting so suddenly as soon as loosened from the rock. Upon examination he appears to have made a wonderful escape for his boat is pierced in numberless places with bullets. It is to be remarked that Mrs. Peyton, who was the night before delivered of an infant, which was unfortunately killed upon the hurry and confusion consequent upon such a disaster, assisted them, being frequently exposed to wet and cold. . . . Their clothes were very much cut with bullets, especially Mrs. Jennings's.

Of the three men who deserted, while the women stood by under fire, the negro was drowned and Jennings's son and the other young man were captured by the Chickamaugans. The latter was burned at the stake. Young Jennings was to have shared the same fate; but a trader in the village, learning that the boy was known to John Sevier, ransomed him by a large payment of goods, as a return for an act of kindness Sevier had once done to him.

Sunday 12th. . . . After running until about 10 o'clock came in sight of the Muscle Shoals. Halted on the northern shore at the appearance of the shoals, in order to search for the signs Captain James Robertson was to make for us at that place . . . that it was practicable for us to go across by land . . . we can find none — from which we conclude that it would not be prudent to make the attempt and are determined, knowing ourselves in such imminent danger, to pursue our journey down the river. . . . When we approached them [the Shoals] they had a dreadful appearance. . . . The water being high made a terrible roaring, which could be heard at some distance, among the driftwood heaped frightfully upon the points of the islands, the current running in every possible direction. Here we did not know how soon we should be dashed to pieces and all our troubles ended at once. Our boats frequently dragged on the bottom and appeared constantly in danger of striking. They warped as much as in a rough sea. But by the hand of Providence we are now preserved from this danger also. I know not the length of this wonderful shoal; it had been represented to me to be twenty-five or thirty miles. If so, we must have descended very rapidly, as indeed we did, for we passed it in about three hours.

On the twentieth the little fleet arrived at the mouth of the Tennessee and the voyagers landed on the bank of the Ohio.

Our situation here is truly disagreeable. The river is very high and the current rapid, our boats not constructed for the purpose of stemming a rapid stream, our provisions exhausted, the crews almost worn down with hunger and fatigue, and know not what distance we have to go or what time it will take us to our place of destination. The scene is rendered still more melancholy as several boats will not attempt to ascend the rapid current. Some intend to descend the Mississippi to Natchez; others are bound for the Illinois — among the rest my son-in-law and daughter. We now part, perhaps to meet no more, for I am determined to pursue my course, happen what will.

Tuesday 21st. Set out and on this day labored very hard and got but little way. . . . Passed the two following days as the former, suffering much from hunger and fatigue.

Friday 24th. About three o'clock came to the mouth of a river which I thought was the Cumberland. Some of the company declared it could not be — it was so much smaller than was expected. . . . We determined however to make the trial, pushed up some distance and encamped for the night.

Saturday 25th. Today we are much encouraged; the river grows wider; . . . we are now convinced it is the Cumberland . . . .

Sunday 26th . . . procured some buffalo meat; though poor it was palatable.

Friday 31st . . . met with Colonel Richard Henderson, who is running the line between Virginia and North Carolina. At this meeting we were much rejoiced. He gave us every information we wished, and further informed us that he had purchased a quantity of corn in Kentucky, to be shipped at the Falls of Ohio for the use of the Cumberland settlement. We are now without bread and are compelled to hunt the buffalo to preserve life. . . .

Monday, April 24th. This day we arrived at our journey's end at the Big Salt Lick, where we have the pleasure of finding Captain Robertson and his company. It is a source of satisfaction to us to be enabled to restore to him and others their families and friends, who were entrusted to our care, and who, sometime since, perhaps, despaired of ever meeting again. . . .

Past the camps of the Chickamaugans — who were retreating farther and farther down the twisting flood, seeking a last standing ground in the giant caves by the Tennessee — these white voyagers had steered their pirogues. Near Robertson's station, where they landed after having traversed

the triangle of the three great rivers which en-
close the larger part of western Tennessee, stood a
crumbling trading house marking the defeat of a
Frenchman who had, one time, sailed in from the
Ohio to establish an outpost of his nation there.
At a little distance were the ruins of a rude fort
cast up by the Cherokees in the days when the re-
doubtable Chickasaws had driven them from the
pleasant shores of the western waters.   Under the
towering forest growth lay vast burial mounds
and the sunken foundations of walled towns, telling of a departed race which had once flashed its
rude paddles and had its dream of permanence
along the courses of these great waterways.   Now
another tribe had come to dream that dream
anew. Already its primitive keels had traced
the opening lines of its history on the face of the
immemorial rivers.

ISAAC SHELBY

Painting on wood by Matthew Harris Jouett, owned (1916), by William R. Shelby, Grand Rapids, Michigan. Photograph in the collections of Archibald Henderson.

CHAPTER IX

KING'S MOUNTAIN

ABOUT the time when James Robertson went from Watauga to fling out the frontier line three hundred miles farther westward, the British took Savannah. In 1780 they took Charleston and Augusta, and overran Georgia. Augusta was the point where the old trading path forked north and west, and it was the key to the Back Country and the overhill domain. In Georgia and the Back Country of South Carolina there were many Tories ready to rally to the King's standard whenever a King's officer should carry it through their midst. A large number of these Tories were Scotch, chiefly from the Highlands. In fact, as we have seen, Scotch blood predominated among the racial streams in the Back Country from Georgia to Pennsylvania. Now, to insure a triumphant march northward for Cornwallis and his royal troops, these sons of Scotland must be gathered together,

195

the loyal encouraged and those of rebellious tendencies converted, and they must be drilled and turned to account. This task, if it were to be accomplished successfully, must be entrusted to an officer with positive qualifications, one who would command respect, whose personal address would attract men and disarm opposition, and especially one who could go as a Scot among his own clan. Cornwallis found his man in Major Patrick Ferguson.

Ferguson was a Highlander, a son of Lord Pitfour of Aberdeen, and thirty-six years of age. He was of short stature for a Highlander — about five feet eight — lean and dark, with straight black hair. He had a serious unhandsome countenance which, at casual glance, might not arrest attention; but when he spoke he became magnetic, by reason of the intelligence and innate force that gleamed in his eyes and the convincing sincerity of his manner. He was admired and respected by his brother officers and by the commanders under whom he had served, and he was loved by his men.

He had seen his first service in the Seven Years' War, having joined the British army in Flanders at the age of fifteen; and he had early distinguished himself for courage and coolness. In 1768, as a captain of infantry, he quelled an insurrection of the natives on the island of St. Vincent in the West Indies. Later, at Woolwich, he took up the scientific study of his profession of arms. He not only became a crack shot, but he invented a new type of rifle which he could load at the breach without ramrod and so quickly as to fire seven times in a minute. Generals and statesmen attended his exhibitions of shooting; and even the King rode over at the head of his guards to watch Ferguson rapidly loading and firing.

In America under Cornwallis, Ferguson had the reputation of being the best shot in the army; and it was soon said that, in his quickness at loading and firing, he excelled the most expert American frontiersman. Eyewitnesses have left their testimony that, seeing a bird alight on a bough or rail, he would drop his bridle rein, draw his pistol, toss it in the air, catch and aim it as it fell, and shoot the bird's head off. He was given command of a corps of picked riflemen; and in the Battle of the Brandywine in 1777 he rendered services which won acclaim from the whole army. For the honor of that day's service to his King, Ferguson paid what from him, with his passion for the rifle, must have been the dearest price that could have been demanded. His right arm was shattered, and for the remaining three years of his short life it hung useless at his side. Yet he took up swordplay and attained a remarkable degree of skill as a left-handed swordsman.

Such was Ferguson, the soldier. What of the man? For he has been pictured as a wolf and a fiend and a coward by early chroniclers, who evidently felt that they were adding to the virtue of those who fought in defense of liberty by representing all their foes as personally odious. We can read his quality of manhood in a few lines of the letter he sent to his kinsman, the noted Dr. Adam Ferguson, about an incident that occurred at Chads Ford. As he was lying with his men in the woods, in front of Knyphausen's army, so he relates, he saw two American officers ride out. He describes their dress minutely. One was in hussar uniform. The other was in a dark green and blue uniform with a high cocked hat and was mounted on a bay horse:

I ordered three good shots to steal near to and fire at them; but the idea disgusting me, I recalled the order. The hussar in retiring made a circuit, but the other passed within a hundred yards of us, upon which I advanced from the wood towards him. Upon my calling he stopped; but after looking at me he proceeded. I again drew his attention and made signs to him to stop, levelling my piece at him; but he slowly cantered away. As I was within that distance, at which, in the quickest firing, I could have lodged half a dozen balls in or about him before he was out of my reach, I had only to determine. But it was not pleasant to fire at the back of an unoffending individual who was acquitting himself very coolly of his duty — so I let him alone. The day after, I had been telling this story to some wounded officers, who lay in the same room with me, when one of the surgeons who had been dressing the wounded rebel officers came in and told us that they had been informing him that General Washington was all the morning with the light troops, and only attended by a French officer in hussar dress, he himself dressed and mounted in every point as above described. *I am not sorry that I did not know at the time who it was.*[1]

Ferguson had his code towards the foe's women also. On one occasion when he was assisting in an action carried out by Hessians and Dragoons, he learned that some American women had been shamefully maltreated. He went in a white fury

[1] Doubt that the officer in question was Washington was expressed by James Fenimore Cooper. Cooper stated that Major De Lancey, his father-in-law, was binding Ferguson's arm at the time when the two officers were seen and Ferguson recalled the order to fire, and that De Lancey said he believed the officer was Count Pulaski. But, as Ferguson, according to his own account, "leveled his piece" at the officer, his arm evidently was not wounded until later in the day. The probability is that Ferguson's version, written in a private letter to his relative, is correct as to the facts, whatever may be conjectured as to the identity of the officer. See Draper's *King's Mountain and its Heroes*, pp. 52–54.

to the colonel in command, and demanded that the men who had so disgraced their uniforms instantly be put to death.

In rallying the loyalists of the Back Country of Georgia and the Carolinas, Ferguson was very successful. He was presently in command of a thousand or more men, including small detachments of loyalists from New York and New Jersey, under American-born officers such as De Peyster and Allaire. There were good honest men among the loyalists and there were also rough and vicious men out for spoils — which was true as well of the Whigs or Patriots from the same counties. Among the rough element were Tory banditti from the overmountain region. It is to be gathered from Ferguson's records that he did not think any too highly of some of his new recruits, but he set to work with all energy to make them useful.

The American Patriots hastily prepared to oppose him. Colonel Charles McDowell of Burke County, North Carolina, with a small force of militia was just south of the line at a point on the Broad River when he heard that Ferguson was sweeping on northward. In haste he sent a call for help across the mountains to Sevier and Shelby. Sevier had his hands full at Watauga, but he dispatched two hundred of his troops; and Isaac Shelby, with a similar force from Sullivan County crossed the mountains to McDowell's assistance. These "overmountain men" or "backwater men," as they were called east of the hills, were trained in Sevier's method of Indian warfare — the secret approach through the dark, the swift dash, and the swifter flight. "Fight strong and run away fast" was the Indian motto, as their women had often been heard to call it after the red men as they ran yelling to fall on the whites. The frontiersmen had adapted the motto to fit their case, as they had also made their own the Indian tactics of ambuscade and surprise attacks at dawn. To sleep, or ride if needs must, by night, and to fight by day and make off, was to them a reasonable soldier's life.

But Ferguson was a night marauder. The terror of his name, which grew among the Whigs of the Back Country until the wildest legends about his ferocity were current, was due chiefly to a habit he had of pouncing on his foes in the middle of the night and pulling them out of bed to give fight or die. It was generally both fight and die, for these dark adventures of his were particularly successful. Ferguson knew no neutrals or conscientious objectors; any man who would not carry arms for the King was a traitor, and his life and goods were forfeit. A report of his reads: "The attack being made at night, no quarter could be given." Hence his wolfish fame. "Werewolf" would have been a fit name for him for, though he was a wolf at night, in the daylight he was a man and, as we have seen, a chivalrous one.

In the guerrilla fighting that went on for a brief time between the overmountain men and various detachments of Ferguson's forces, sometimes one side, sometimes the other, won the heat. But the field remained open. Neither side could claim the mastery. In a minor engagement fought at Musgrove's Mill on the Enoree, Shelby's command came off victor and was about to pursue the enemy towards Ninety-Six when a messenger from McDowell galloped madly into camp with word of General Gates's crushing defeat at Camden. This was a warning for Shelby's guerrillas to flee as birds to their mountains, or Ferguson would cut them off from the north and wedge them in between his own force and the victorious Cornwallis. McDowell's men, also on the run for safety, joined them. For forty-eight hours without food or rest they rode a race with Ferguson, who kept hard on their trail until they disappeared into the mystery of the winding mountain paths they alone knew.

Ferguson reached the gap where they had swerved into the towering hills only half an hour after their horses' hoofs had pounded across it. Here he turned back. His troops were exhausted from the all-night ride and, in any case, there were not enough of them to enable him to cross the mountains and give the Watauga men battle on their own ground with a fair promise of victory. So keeping east of the hills but still close to them, Ferguson turned into Burke County, North Carolina. He sat him down in Gilbert Town (present Lincolnton, Lincoln County) at the foot of the Blue Ridge and indited a letter to the "Back Water Men," telling them that if they did not lay down their arms and return to their rightful allegiance, he would come over their hills and raze their settlements and hang their leaders. He paroled a kinsman of Shelby's, whom he had taken prisoner in the chase, and sent him home with the letter. Then he set about his usual business of gathering up Tories and making soldiers of them, and of hunting down rebels.

One of the "rebels" was a certain Captain Lytle. When Ferguson drew up at Lytle's door, Lytle had

already made his escape; but Mrs. Lytle was there.
She was a very handsome woman and she had
dressed herself in her best to receive Ferguson, who
was reported a gallant as well as a wolf. After a
few spirited passages between the lady in the doorway and the officer on the white horse before it,
the latter advised Mrs. Lytle to use her influence
to bring her husband back to his duty. She became grave then and answered that her husband
would never turn traitor to his country. Ferguson
frowned at the word "traitor," but presently he
said: "Madam, I admire you as the handsomest
woman I have seen in North Carolina. I even
half way admire your zeal in a bad cause. But
take my word for it, the rebellion has had its day
and is now virtually put down. Give my regards
to Captain Lytle and tell him to come in. He will
not be asked to compromise his honor. His verbal
pledge not again to take up arms against the King
is all that will be asked of him."[1]

This was another phase of the character of the
one-armed Highlander whose final challenge to the
back water men was now being considered in every
log cabin beyond the hills. A man who would not
shoot an enemy in the back, who was ready to put

[1] Draper, *King's Mountain and its Heroes*, pp. 151-53.

the same faith in another soldier's honor which
he knew was due to his own, yet in battle a wolfish fighter who leaped through the dark to give
no quarter and to take none — he was fit chal-
lenger to those other mountaineers who also had a
chivalry of their own, albeit they too were wolves
of war.

When Shelby on the Holston received Ferguson's
pungent letter, he flung himself on his horse and
rode posthaste to Watauga to consult with Sevier.
He found the bank of the Nolichucky teeming
with merrymakers. Nolichucky Jack was giving
an immense barbecue and a horse race. Without
letting the festival crowd have an inkling of the
serious nature of Shelby's errand, the two men
drew apart to confer. It is said to have been Sevier's idea that they should muster the forces of
the western country and go in search of Ferguson
ere the latter should be able to get sufficient reinforcements to cross the mountains. Sevier, like
Ferguson, always preferred to seek his foe, knowing
well the advantage of the offensive. Messengers
were sent to Colonel William Campbell of the
Virginia settlements on the Clinch, asking his aid.
Campbell at first refused, thinking it better to
fortify the positions they held and let Ferguson

come and put the mountains between himself and Cornwallis. On receipt of a second message, however, he concurred. The call to arms was heard up and down the valleys, and the frontiersmen poured into Watauga. The overhill men were augmented by McDowell's troops from Burke County, who had dashed over the mountains a few weeks before in their escape from Ferguson.

At daybreak on the 26th of September they mustered at the Sycamore Shoals on the Watauga, over a thousand strong. It was a different picture they made from that other great gathering at the same spot when Henderson had made his purchase in money of the Dark and Bloody Ground, and Sevier and Robertson had bought for the Wataugans this strip of Tennessee. There were no Indians in this picture. Dragging Canoe, who had uttered his bloody prophecy, had by these very men been driven far south into the caves of the Tennessee River. But the Indian prophecy still hung over them, and in this day with a heavier menace. Not with money, now, were they to seal their purchase of the free land by the western waters. There had been no women in that other picture, only the white men who were going forward to open the way and the red men who were

retreating. But in this picture there were women
— wives and children, mothers, sisters, and sweet-
hearts. All the women of the settlement were
there at this daybreak muster to cheer on their
way the men who were going out to battle that
they might keep the way of liberty open not for
men only but for women and children also. And
the battle to which the men were now going forth
must be fought against Back Country men of their
own stripe under a leader who, in other circumstances, might well have been one of themselves —
a primitive spirit of hardy mountain stock, who,
having once taken his stand, would not barter and
would not retreat.

"With the Sword of the Lord and of Gideon!"
cried their pastor, the Reverend Samuel Doak,
with upraised hands, as the mountaineers swung
into their saddles. And it is said that all the
women took up his words and cried again and
again, "With the sword of the Lord and of our
Gideons!" To the shouts of their women, as bugles
on the wind of dawn, the buckskin-shirted army
dashed out upon the mountain trail.

The warriors' equipment included rifles and ammunition, tomahawks, knives, shot pouches, a knap-
sack, and a blanket for each man. Their uniforms

were leggings, breeches, and long loose shirts of gayly fringed deerskin, or of the linsey-woolsey spun by their women. Their hunting shirts were bound in at the waist by bright-colored linsey sashes tied behind in a bow. They wore moccasins for footgear, and on their heads high fur or deerskin caps trimmed with colored bands of raveled cloth. Around their necks hung their powder-horns ornamented with their own rude carvings.

On the first day they drove along with them a number of beeves but, finding that the cattle impeded the march, they left them behind on the mountain side. Their provisions thereafter were wild game and the small supply each man carried of mixed corn meal and maple sugar. For drink, they had the hill streams.

They passed upward between Roan and Yellow mountains to the top of the range. Here, on the bald summit, where the loose snow lay to their ankles, they halted for drill and rifle practice. When Sevier called up his men, he discovered that two were missing. He suspected at once that they had slipped away to carry warning to Ferguson, for Watauga was known to be infested with Tories. Two problems now confronted the mountaineers. They must increase the speed of their march, so

that Ferguson should not have time to get reinforcements from Cornwallis; and they must make
that extra speed by another trail than they had
intended taking so that they themselves could not
be intercepted before they had picked up the Back
Country militia under Colonels Cleveland, Hamp-
bright, Chronicle, and Williams, who were moving
to join them. We are not told who took the lead
when they left the known trail, but we may suppose it was Sevier and his Wataugans, for the making of new warpaths and wild riding were two of
the things which distinguished Nolichucky Jack's
leadership. Down the steep side of the mountain,
finding their way as they plunged, went the overhill men. They crossed the Blue Ridge at Gillespie's Gap and pushed on to Quaker Meadows,
where Colonel Cleveland with 350 men swung into
their column. Along their route, the Back Country
Patriots with their rifles came out from the little
hamlets and the farms and joined them.

They now had an army of perhaps fifteen hundred men but no commanding officer. Thus far,
on the march, the four colonels had conferred
together and agreed as to procedure; or, in real-
ity, the influence of Sevier and Shelby, who had
planned the enterprise and who seem always to

14

have acted in unison, had swayed the others. It would be, however, manifestly improper to go into battle without a real general. Something must be done. McDowell volunteered to carry a letter explaining their need to General Gates, who had escaped with some of his staff into North Carolina and was not far off. It then occurred to Sevier and Shelby, evidently for the first time, that Gates, on receiving such a request, might well ask why the Governor of North Carolina, as the military head of the State, had not provided a commander. The truth is that Sevier and Shelby had been so busy drumming up the militia and planning their campaign that they had found no time to consult the Governor. Moreover, the means whereby the expedition had been financed might not have appealed to the chief executive. After finding it impossible to raise sufficient funds on his personal credit, Sevier had appropriated the entry money in the government land office to the business in hand — with the good will of the entry taker, who was a patriotic man, although, as he had pointed out, he could not, *officially*, hand over the money. Things being as they were, no doubt Nolichucky Jack felt that an interview with the Governor had better be deferred until after the capture of Ferguson. Hence the tenor of this communication to General Gates:

As we have at this time called out our militia without any orders from the Executive of our different States and with the view of expelling the Enemy out of this part of the Country, we think such a body of men worthy of your attention and would request you to send a General Officer immediately to take the command. . . . All our Troops being Militia and but little acquainted with discipline, we could wish him to be a Gentleman of address, and able to keep up a proper discipline *without disgusting the soldiery.*

For some unknown reason — unless it might be the wording of this letter! — no officer was sent in reply. Shelby then suggested that, since all the officers but Campbell were North Carolinians and, therefore, no one of them could be promoted without arousing the jealousy of the others, Campbell, as the only Virginian, was the appropriate choice. The sweet reasonableness of selecting a commander from such a motive appealed to all, and Campbell became a general in fact if not in name! Shelby's principal aim, however, had been to get rid of McDowell, who, as their senior, would naturally expect to command and whom he considered "too far advanced in life and too inactive" for such an enterprise. At this time McDowell must have been nearly thirty-nine; and Shelby, who was just thirty, wisely refused to risk the campaign under a general who was in his dotage!

News of the frontiersmen's approach, with their augmented force, now numbering between sixteen and eighteen hundred, had reached Ferguson by the two Tories who had deserted from Sevier's troops. Ferguson thereupon had made all haste out of Gilbert Town and was marching southward to get in touch with Cornwallis. His force was much reduced, as some of his men were in pursuit of Elijah Clarke towards Augusta and a number of his other Tories were on furlough. As he passed through the Back Country he posted a notice calling on the loyalists to join him. If the overmountain men felt that they were out on a wolf hunt, Ferguson's proclamation shows what the wolf thought of his hunters.

To the Inhabitants of North Carolina.

GENTLEMEN: Unless you wish to be eat up by an innundation of barbarians, who have begun by murdering an unarmed son before the aged father, and afterwards lopped off his arms, and who by their shocking cruelties and irregularities give the best proof of their cowardice and want of discipline: I say if you wish to be pinioned, robbed and murdered, and see your wives and daughters in four days, abused by the dregs of mankind — in

short if you wish to deserve to live and bear the name of
men, grasp your arms in a moment and run to camp.

The Back Water men have crossed the mountains:
McDowell, Hampton, Shelby, and Cleveland are at their
head, so that you know what you have to depend upon.
If you choose to be degraded forever and ever by a
set of mongrels, say so at once, and let your women
turn their backs upon you, and look out for real men to
protect them.

PAT. FERGUSON, Major 71st Regiment.[1]

Ferguson's force has been estimated at about
eleven hundred men, but it is likely that this esti-
mate does not take the absentees into consideration. In the diary of Lieutenant Allaire, one of his
officers, the number is given as only eight hundred.
Because of the state of his army, chroniclers have
found Ferguson's movements, after leaving Gilbert Town, difficult to explain. It has been pointed
out that he could easily have escaped, for he had
plenty of time, and Charlotte, Cornwallis's head-
quarters, was only sixty miles distant. We have
seen something of Ferguson's quality, however, and
we may simply take it that he did not want to
escape. He had been planning to cross the high
hills — to him, the Highlander, no barrier but a
challenge — to fight these men. Now that they

[1] Draper, *King's Mountain and its Heroes*, p. 204.

had taken the initiative he would not show them his back. He craved the battle. So he sent out runners to the main army and rode on along the eastern base of the mountains, seeking a favorable site to go into camp and wait for Cornwallis's aid. On the 6th of October he reached the southern end of the King's Mountain ridge, in South Carolina, about half a mile south of the northern boundary. Here a rocky, semi-isolated spur juts out from the ridge, its summit — a table-land about six hundred yards long and one hundred and twenty wide at its northern end — rising not more than sixty feet above the surrounding country. On the summit Ferguson pitched his camp.

The hill was a natural fortress, its sides forested, its bald top protected by rocks and bowlders. All the approaches led through dense forest. An enemy force, passing through the immediate, wooded territory, might easily fail to discover a small army nesting sixty feet above the shrouding leafage. Word was evidently brought to Ferguson here, telling him the now augmented number of his foe, for he dispatched another emissary to Cornwallis with a letter stating the number of his own troops and urging full and immediate assistance.

Meanwhile the frontiersmen had halted at the

Cowpens. There they feasted royally off roasted cattle and corn belonging to the loyalist who owned the Cowpens. It is said that they mowed his fifty acres of corn in an hour. And here one of their spies, in the assumed rôle of a Tory, learned Ferguson's plans, his approximate force, his route, and his system of communication with Cornwallis. The officers now held council and determined to take a detachment of the hardiest and fleetest horsemen and sweep down on the enemy before aid could reach him. About nine o'clock that evening, according to Shelby's report, 910 mounted men set off at full speed, leaving the main body of horse and foot to follow after at their best pace.

Rain poured down on them all that night as they rode. At daybreak they crossed the Broad at Cherokee Ford and dashed on in the drenching rain all the forenoon. They kept their firearms and powder dry by wrapping them in their knapsacks, blankets, and hunting shirts. The downpour had so churned up the soil that many of the horses mired, but they were pulled out and whipped forward again. The wild horsemen made no halt for food or rest. Within two miles of King's Mountain they captured Ferguson's messenger with the letter that told of his desperate situation. They asked this man how they should know Ferguson. He told them that Ferguson was in full uniform but wore a checkered shirt or dust cloak over it. This was not the only messenger of Ferguson's who failed to carry through. The men he had sent out previously had been followed and, to escape capture or death, they had been obliged to lie in hiding, so that they did not reach Cornwallis until the day of the battle.

At three o'clock on the afternoon of the 7th of October, the overmountain men were in the forest at the base of the hill. The rain had ceased and the sun was shining. They dismounted and tethered their steaming horses. Orders were given that every man was to "throw the priming out of his pan, pick his touchhole, prime anew, examine bullets and see that everything was in readiness for battle." The plan of battle agreed on was to surround the hill, hold the enemy on the top and, themselves screened by the trees, keep pouring in their fire. There was a good chance that most of the answering fire would go over their heads.

As Shelby's men crossed a gap in the woods, the outposts on the hill discovered their presence and sounded the alarm. Ferguson sprang to horse, blowing his silver whistle to call his men to attack.

His riflemen poured fire into Shelby's contingent, but meanwhile the frontiersmen on the other sides were creeping up, and presently a circle of fire burst upon the hill. With fixed bayonets, some of Ferguson's men charged down the face of the slope, against the advancing foe, only to be shot in the back as they charged. Still time and time again they charged; the overhill men reeled and retreated; but always their comrades took toll with their rifles; Ferguson's men, preparing for a mounted charge, were shot even as they swung to their saddles. Ferguson, with his customary indifference to danger, rode up and down in front of his line blowing his whistle to encourage his men. "Huzza, brave boys! The day is our own!" Thus he was heard to shout above the triumphant war whoops of the circling foe, surging higher and higher about the hill.

But there were others in his band who knew the fight was lost. The overmountain men saw two white handkerchiefs, affixed to bayonets, raised above the rocks; and then they saw Ferguson dash by and slash them down with his sword. Two horses were shot under Ferguson in the latter part of the action; but he mounted a third and rode again into the thick of the fray.

Suddenly the cry spread among the attacking troops that the British officer, Tarleton, had come to Ferguson's rescue; and the mountaineers began to give way. But it was only the galloping horses of their own comrades; Tarleton had not come. Nolichucky Jack spurred out in front of his men and rode along the line. Fired by his courage they sounded the war whoop again and renewed the attack with fury.

"These are the same yelling devils that were at Musgrove's Mill," said Captain De Peyster to Ferguson.

Now Shelby and Sevier, leading his Wataugans, had reached the summit. The firing circle pressed in. The buckskin-shirted warriors leaped the rocky barriers, swinging their tomahawks and long knives. Again the white handkerchiefs fluttered. Ferguson saw that the morale of his troops was shattered.

"Surrender," De Peyster, his second in command, begged of him.

"Surrender to those damned banditti? Never!" Ferguson turned his horse's head downhill and charged into the Wataugans, hacking right and left with his sword till it was broken at the hilt. A dozen rifles were leveled at him. An iron muzzle pushed at his breast, but the powder flashed in the pan. He swerved and struck at the rifleman with his broken hilt. But the other guns aimed at him spoke; and Ferguson's body jerked from the saddle pierced by eight bullets. Men seized the bridle of the frenzied horse, plunging on with his dead master dragging from the stirrup.

The battle had lasted less than an hour. After Ferguson fell, De Peyster advanced with a white flag and surrendered his sword to Campbell. Other white flags waved along the hilltop. But the killing did not yet cease. It is said that many of the mountaineers did not know the significance of the white flag. Sevier's sixteen-year-old son, having heard that his father had fallen, kept on furiously loading and firing until presently he saw Sevier ride in among the troops and command them to stop shooting men who had surrendered and thrown down their arms.

The victors made a bonfire of the enemy's baggage wagons and supplies. Then they killed some of his beeves and cooked them; they had had neither food nor sleep for eighteen hours. They dug shallow trenches for the dead and scattered the loose earth over them. Ferguson's body, stripped of its uniform and boots and wrapped in a beef hide, was thrown into one of these ditches by the men detailed to the burial work, while the officers divided his personal effects among themselves.

The triumphant army turned homeward as the dusk descended. The uninjured prisoners and the wounded who were able to walk were marched off carrying their empty firearms. The badly wounded were left lying where they had fallen.

At Bickerstaff's Old Fields in Rutherford County the frontiersmen halted; and here they selected thirty of their prisoners to be hanged. They swung them aloft, by torchlight, three at a time, until nine had gone to their last account. Then Sevier interposed; and, with Shelby's added authority, saved the other twenty-one. Among those who thus weighted the gallows tree were some of the Tory brigands from Watauga; but not all the victims were of this character. Some of the troops would have wreaked vengeance on the two Tories from Sevier's command who had betrayed their army plans to Ferguson; but Sevier claimed them as under his jurisdiction and refused consent. Nolichucky Jack dealt humanely by his foes. To the coarse and brutish Cleveland, now astride of Ferguson's horse and wearing his sash, and to the three hundred who followed him, may no doubt be laid the worst excesses of the battle's afterpiece.

Victors and vanquished drove on in the dark, close to the great flank of hills. From where King's Mountain, strewn with dead and dying, reared its black shape like some rudely hewn tomb of a primordial age when titans strove together, perhaps to the ears of the marching men came faintly through the night's stillness the howl of a wolf and the answering chorus of the pack. For the wolves came down to King's Mountain from all the surrounding hills, following the scent of blood, and made their lair where the Werewolf had fallen. The scene of the mountaineers' victory, which marked the turn of the tide for the Revolution, became for years the chief resort of wolf hunters from both the Carolinas.

The importance of the overmountain men's victory lay in what it achieved for the cause of Independence. King's Mountain was the prelude to Cornwallis's defeat. It heartened the Southern Patriots, until then cast down by Gates's disaster. To the British the death of Ferguson was an irreparable loss because of its depressing effect on the Back Country Tories. King's Mountain, indeed, broke the Tory spirit. Seven days after the battle General Nathanael Greene succeeded to the command of the Southern Patriot army which Gates had led to defeat. Greene's genius met the rising tide of the Patriots' courage and hope and took it at the flood. His strategy, in dividing his army and thereby compelling the division of Cornwallis's force, led to Daniel Morgan's victory at the Cowpens, in the Back Country of South Carolina, on January 17, 1781 — another frontiersmen's triumph. Though the British won the next engagement between Greene and Cornwallis — the battle of Guilford Court House in the North Carolina Back Country, on the 15th of March — Greene made them pay so dearly for their victory that Tarleton called it "the pledge of ultimate defeat"; and, three days later, Cornwallis was retreating towards Wilmington. In a sense, then, King's Mountain was the pivot of the war's revolving stage, which swung the British from their succession of victories towards the surrender at Yorktown.

Shelby, Campbell, and Cleveland escorted the prisoners to Virginia. Sevier, with his men, rode home to Watauga. When the prisoners had been delivered to the authorities in Virginia, the Holston men also turned homeward through the hills. Their route lay down through the Clinch and Holston valleys to the settlement at the base of the

mountains. Sevier and his Wataugans had gone by
Gillespie's Gap, over the pathway that hung like a
narrow ribbon about the breast of Roan Mountain, lifting its crest in dignified isolation sixty-
three hundred feet above the levels. The "Unakas"
was the name the Cherokees had given to those
white men who first invaded their hills; and the
Unakas is the name that white men at last gave
to the mountains.

Great companies of men were to come over the
mountain paths on their way to the Mississippi
country and beyond; and with them, as we know,
were to go many of these mountain men, to pass
away with their customs in the transformations
that come with progress. But there were others
who clung to these hills. They were of several
stocks — English, Scotch, Highlanders, Ulstermen, who mingled by marriage and sometimes took
their mates from among the handsome maids of
the Cherokees. They spread from the Unakas of
Tennessee into the Cumberland Mountains of Kentucky; and they have remained to this day what
they were then, a primitive folk of strong and
fiery men and brave women living as their forefathers of Watauga and Holston lived. In the log
cabins in those mountains today are heard the

same ballads, sung still to the dulcimer, that entertained the earliest settlers. The women still turn the old-fashioned spinning wheels. The code of the men is still the code learned perhaps from the Gaels — the code of the oath and the feud and the open door to the stranger. Or were these, the ethical tenets of almost all uncorrupted primitive tribes, transmitted from the Indian strain and association? Their young people marry at boy and girl ages, as the pioneers did, and their wedding festivities are the same as those which made rejoicing at the first marriage in Watauga. Their common speech today contains words that have been obsolete in England for a hundred years.

Thrice have the mountain men come down again from their fastnesses to war for America since the day of King's Mountain and thrice they have acquitted themselves so that their deeds are noted in history. A souvenir of their part in the War of 1812 at the Battle of the Thames is kept in one of the favorite names for mountain girls — "Lake Erie." In the Civil War many volunteers from the free, non-slaveholding mountain regions of Kentucky and Tennessee joined the Union Army, and it is said that they exceeded all others in stature and physical development. And in our own day their sons again came down from the mountains to carry the torch of Liberty overseas, and to show the white stars in their flag side by side with the ancient cross in the flag of England against which their forefathers fought.

15

CHAPTER X

AFTER King's Mountain, Sevier reached home just in time to fend off a Cherokee attack on Watauga. Again warning had come to the settlements that the Indians were about to descend upon them. Sevier set out at once to meet the red invaders. Learning from his scouts that the Indians were near he went into ambush with his troops disposed in the figure of a half-moon, the favorite Indian formation. He then sent out a small body of men to fire on the Indians and make a scampering retreat, to lure the enemy on. The maneuver was so well planned and the ground so well chosen that the Indian war party would probably have been annihilated but for the delay of an officer at one horn of the half-moon in bringing his troops into play. Through the gap thus made the Indians escaped, with a loss of seventeen of their number. The delinquent officer was Jonathan Tipton, younger brother of Colonel John Tipton, of whom we shall hear later. It is possible that from this event dates the Tiptons' feud with Sevier, which supplies one of the breeziest pages in the story of early Tennessee.

Not content with putting the marauders to flight, Sevier pressed on after them, burned several of the upper towns, and took prisoner a number of women and children, thus putting the red warriors to the depth of shame, for the Indians never deserted their women in battle. The chiefs at once sued for peace. But they had made peace often before. Sevier drove down upon the Hiwassee towns, meanwhile proclaiming that those among the tribe who were friendly might send their families to the white settlement, where they would be fed and cared for until a sound peace should be assured. He also threatened to continue to make war until his enemies were wiped out, their town sites a heap of blackened ruins, and their whole country in possession of the whites, unless they bound themselves to an enduring peace.

Having compelled the submission of the Otari and Hiwassee towns, yet finding that depredations still continued, Sevier determined to invade the group of towns hidden in the mountain fastnesses near the headwaters of the Little Tennessee where, deeming themselves inaccessible except by their own trail, the Cherokees freely plotted mischief and sent out raiding parties. These hill towns lay in the high gorges of the Great Smoky Mountains, 150 miles distant. No one in Watauga had ever been in them except Thomas, the trader, who, however, had reached them from the eastern side of the mountains. With no knowledge of the Indians' path and without a guide, yet nothing daunted, Sevier, late in the summer of 1781 headed his force into the mountains. So steep were some of the slopes they scaled that the men were obliged to dismount and help their horses up. Unexpectedly to themselves perhaps, as well as to the Indians, they descended one morning on a group of villages and destroyed them. Before the fleeing savages could rally, the mountaineers had plunged up the steeps again. Sevier then turned southward into Georgia and inflicted a severe castigation on the tribes along the Coosa River.

When, after thirty days of warfare and mad riding, Sevier arrived at his Bonnie Kate's door on the Nolichucky, he found a messenger from General Greene calling on him for immediate assistance to cut off Cornwallis from his expected retreat through North Carolina. Again he set out, and with two hundred men crossed the mountains and made all speed to Charlotte, in Mecklenburg County, where he learned that Cornwallis had surrendered at Yorktown on October 19, 1781. Under Greene's orders he turned south to the Santee to assist a fellow scion of the Huguenots, General Francis Marion, in the pursuit of Stuart's Britishers. Having driven Stuart into Charleston, Sevier and his active Wataugans returned home, now perhaps looking forward to a rest, which they had surely earned. Once more, however, they were hailed with alarming news. Dragging Canoe had come to life again and was emerging from the caves of the Tennessee with a substantial force of Chickamaugan warriors. Again the Wataugans, augmented by a detachment from Sullivan County, galloped forth, met the red warriors, chastised them heavily, put them to rout, burned their dwellings and provender, and drove them back into their hiding places. For some time after this, the Indians dipped not into the black paint pots of war but were content to streak their humbled countenances with the vermilion of beauty and innocence.

It should be chronicled that Sevier, assisted possibly by other Wataugans, eventually returned to the State of North Carolina the money which he had forcibly borrowed to finance the King's Mountain expedition; and that neither he nor Shelby received any pay for their services, nor asked it. Before Shelby left the Holston in 1782 and moved to Kentucky, of which State he was to become the first Governor, the Assembly of North Carolina passed a resolution of gratitude to the overmountain men in general, and to Sevier and Shelby in particular, for their "very generous and patriotic services" with which the "General Assembly of this State are feelingly impressed." The resolution concluded by urging the recipients of the Assembly's acknowledgments to "continue" in their noble course. In view of what followed, this resolution is interesting!

For some time the overhill pioneers had been growing dissatisfied with the treatment they were receiving from the State, which on the plea of poverty had refused to establish a Superior Court for them and to appoint a prosecutor. As a result, crime was on the increase, and the law-abiding were deprived of the proper legal means to check the lawless. In 1784 when the western soldiers' claims began to reach the Assembly, there to be scrutinized by unkindly eyes, the dissatisfaction increased.

The breasts of the mountain men — the men who had made that spectacular ride to bring Ferguson to his end — were kindled with hot indignation when they heard that they had been publicly assailed as grasping persons who seized on every pretense to "fabricate demands against the Government." Nor were those fiery breasts cooled by further plaints to the effect that the "industry and property" of those east of the hills were "becoming the funds appropriated to discharge the debts" of the Westerners. They might with justice have asked what the industry and property of the Easterners were worth on that day when the overhill men drilled in the snows on the high peak of Yellow Mountain and looked down on Burke County overrun by Ferguson's Tories, and beyond, to Charlotte, where lay Cornwallis.

The North Carolina Assembly did not confine itself to impolite remarks. It proceeded to get rid of what it deemed western rapacity by ceding the whole overmountain territory to the United States, with the proviso that Congress must accept the gift within twelve months. And after passing the Cession Act, North Carolina closed the land office in the undesired domain and nullified all entries made after May 25, 1784. The Cession Act also enabled the State to evade its obligations to the Cherokees in the matter of an expensive consignment of goods to pay for new lands.

This clever stroke of the Assembly's brought about immediate consequences in the region beyond the hills. The Cherokees, who knew nothing about the Assembly's system of political economy but who found their own provokingly upset by the non-arrival of the promised goods, began again to darken the mixture in their paint pots; and they dug up the war hatchet, never indeed so deeply patted down under the dust that it could not be unearthed by a stub of the toe. Needless to say, it was not the thrifty and distant Easterners who felt their anger, but the nearby settlements.

As for the white overhill dwellers, the last straw had been laid on their backs; and it felt like a hickory log. No sooner had the Assembly adjourned than the men of Washington, Sullivan, and Greene counties, which comprised the settled portion of what is now east Tennessee, elected delegates to convene for the purpose of discussing the formation of a new State. They could assert that they were not acting illegally, for in her first constitution North Carolina had made provision for a State beyond the mountains. And necessity compelled them to take steps for their protection. Some of them, and Sevier was of the number, doubted if Congress would accept the costly gift; and the majority realized that during the twelve months which were allowed for the decision they would have no protection from either North Carolina or Congress and would not be able to command their own resources.

In August, 1784, the delegates met at Jonesborough and passed preliminary resolutions, and then adjourned to meet later in the year. The news was soon disseminated through North Carolina and the Assembly convened in October and hastily repealed the Cession Act, voted to establish the District of Washington out of the four counties, and sent word of the altered policy to Sevier, with a commission for himself as Brigadier General. From the steps of the improvised convention hall, before which the delegates had gathered, Sevier read the Assembly's message and advised his neighbors to proceed no further, since North Carolina had of her own accord redressed all their grievances. But for once Nolichucky Jack's followers refused to follow. The adventure too greatly appealed. Obliged to choose between North Carolina and his own people, Sevier's hesitation was short. The State of Frankland, or Land of the Free, was formed; and Nolichucky Jack was elevated to the office of Governor — with a yearly salary of two hundred mink skins.

Perhaps John Tipton had hoped to head the new State, for he had been one of its prime movers and was a delegate to this convention. But when the man whom he hated — apparently for no reason except that other men loved him — assented to the people's will and was appointed to the highest post within their gift, Tipton withdrew, disavowing all connection with Frankland and affirming his loyalty to North Carolina. From this time on, the feud was an open one.

That brief and now forgotten State, Frankland, the Land of the Free, which bequeathed its name as an appellation for America, was founded as Watauga had been founded — to meet the practical needs and aspirations of its people. It will be remembered that one of the things written by Sevier into the only Watauga document extant was that they desired to become "in every way the best members of society." Frankland's aims, as recorded, included the intent to "improve agriculture, perfect manufacturing, *encourage literature* and every thing truly laudable."

The constitution of Frankland, agreed to on the 14th of November, 1785, appeals to us today rather by its spirit than by its practical provisions. "This State shall be called the Commonwealth of Frankland and shall be governed by a General Assembly of the representatives of the freemen of the same, a Governor and Council, and proper courts of justice. . . . The supreme legislative power shall be vested in a single House of Representatives of the freemen of the commonwealth of Frankland. The House of Representatives of the freemen of the State shall consist of persons most noted for wisdom and virtue."

In these exalted desires of the primitive men who held by their rifles and hatchets the land by the western waters, we see the influence of the Reverend Samuel Doak, their pastor, who founded the first church and the first school beyond the great hills. Early in the life of Watauga he had come thither from Princeton, a zealous and broadminded young man, and a sturdy one, too, for he came on foot driving before him a mule laden with books. Legend credits another minister, the Reverend Samuel Houston, with suggesting the name of Frankland, after he had opened the Convention with prayer. It is not surprising to learn that this glorified constitution was presently put aside in favor of one modeled on that of North Carolina.

Sevier persuaded the more radical members of the community to abandon their extreme views and to adopt the laws of North Carolina. However lawless his acts as Governor of a bolting colony may appear, Sevier was essentially a constructive force. His purposes were right, and small motives are not discernible in his record. He might reasonably urge that the Franklanders had only followed the example of North Carolina and the other American States in seceding from the parent body, and for similar causes, for the State's system of taxation had long borne heavily on the overhill men.

The whole transmontane populace welcomed Frankland with enthusiasm. Major Arthur Campbell, of the Virginian settlements, on the Holston, was eager to join. Sevier and his Assembly took the necessary steps to receive the overhill Virginians, provided that the transfer of allegiance could be made with Virginia's consent. Meanwhile he replied in a dignified manner to the pained and menacing expostulations of North Carolina's Governor. North Carolina was bidden to remember the epithets her assemblymen had hurled at the Westerners, which they themselves had by no means forgotten. And was it any wonder that they now doubted the love the parent State professed to feel for them? As for the puerile threat of blood, had their quality really so soon become obliterated from the memory of North Carolina? At this sort of writing, Sevier, who always pulsed hot with emotion and who had a pretty knack in turning a phrase, was more than a match for the Governor of North Carolina, whose prerogatives he had usurped.

The overmountain men no longer needed to complain bitterly of the lack of legal machinery to keep them "the best members of society." They now had courts to spare. Frankland had its courts, its judges, its legislative body, its land office — in fact, a full governmental equipment. North Carolina also performed all the natural functions of political organism, within the western territory. Sevier appointed one David Campbell a judge. Campbell held court in Jonesborough. Ten miles away, in Buffalo, Colonel John Tipton presided for North Carolina. It happened frequently that officers and attendants of the rival law courts met, as they pursued their duties, and whenever they met they fought. The post of sheriff — or sheriffs, for of course there were two — was filled by the biggest and heaviest man and the hardest hitter in the ranks of the warring factions. A favorite game was raiding each other's courts and carrying off the records. Frankland sent William Cocke, later the first senator from Tennessee, to Congress with a memorial, asking Congress to accept the territory North Carolina had offered and to receive it into the Union as a separate State. Congress ignored the plea. It began to appear that North Carolina would be victor in the end; and so there were defections among the Franklanders. Sevier wrote to Benjamin Franklin asking his aid in establishing the status of Frankland; and, with a graceful flourish of his ready pen, changed the new State's name to Franklin by way of reinforcing his arguments. But the old philosopher, more expert than Sevier in diplomatic calligraphy, only acknowledged the compliment and advised the State of Franklin to make peace with North Carolina.

Sevier then appealed for aid and recognition to the Governor of Georgia, who had previously appointed him Brigadier General of militia. But the Governor of Georgia also avoided giving the recognition requested, though he earnestly besought Sevier to come down and settle the Creeks for him. There were others who sent pleas to Sevier, the

warrior, to save them from the savages. One of
the writers who addressed him did not fear to say
"Your Excellency," nor to accord Nolichucky Jack
the whole dignity of the purple in appealing to
him as the only man possessing the will and the
power to prevent the isolated settlements on the
Cumberland from being wiped out. That writer
was his old friend, James Robertson.

In 1787, while Sevier was on the frontier of
Greene County, defending it from Indians, the
legal forces of North Carolina swooped down on
his estate and took possession of his negroes. It
was Tipton who represented the law; and Tipton
carried off the Governor's slaves to his own estate.
When Nolichucky Jack came home and found that
his enemy had stripped him, he was in a towering
rage. With a body of his troops and one small
cannon, he marched to Tipton's house and besieged
it, threatening a bombardment. He did not, however, fire into the dwelling, though he placed some
shots about it and in the extreme corners. This
opéra bouffe siege endured for several days, until
Tipton was reinforced by some of his own clique.
Then Tipton sallied forth and attacked the be-
siegers, who hastily scattered rather than engage
in a sanguinary fight with their neighbors. Tipton

captured Sevier's two elder sons and was only restrained from hanging them on being informed that two of his own sons were at that moment in Sevier's hands.

In March, 1788, the State of Franklin went into eclipse. Sevier was overthrown by the authorities of North Carolina. Most of the officials who had served under him were soothed by being reappointed to their old positions. Tipton's star was now in the ascendant, for his enemy was to be made the vicarious sacrifice for the sins of all whom he had "led astray." Presently David Campbell, still graciously permitted to preside over the Superior Court, received from the Governor of North Carolina the following letter:

SIR: It has been represented to the Executive that John Sevier, who styles himself Captain-General of the State of Franklin, has been guilty of high treason in levying troops to oppose the laws and government of the State. . . . You will issue your warrant to apprehend the said John Sevier, and in case he cannot be sufficiently secured for trial in the District of Washington, order him to be committed to the public gaol.

The judge's authority was to be exercised after he had examined the "affidavits of credible persons." Campbell's judicial opinion seems to have been that any affidavit *against* "the said John

Sevier" could not be made by a "credible person."
He refused to issue the warrant. Tipton's friend,
Spencer, who had been North Carolina's judge
of the Superior Court in the West and who was
sharing that honor now with Campbell, issued the
warrant and sent Tipton to make the arrest.

Sevier was at the Widow Brown's inn with some
of his men when Tipton at last came up with him.
It was early morning. Tipton and his posse were
about to enter when the portly and dauntless
widow, surmising their errand, drew her chair into
the doorway, plumped herself down in it, and refused to budge for all the writs in North Carolina.
Tipton blustered and the widow rocked. The altercation awakened Sevier. He dressed hurriedly
and came down. As soon as he presented himself
on the porch, Tipton thrust his pistol against his
body, evidently with intent to fire if Sevier made
signs of resistance. Sevier's furious followers were
not disposed to let him be taken without a fight,
but he admonished them to respect the law, and requested that they would inform Bonnie Kate of his
predicament. Then, debonair as ever, with perhaps
a tinge of contempt at the corners of his mouth, he
held out his wrists for the manacles which Tipton
insisted on fastening upon them.

It was not likely that any jail in the western country could hold Nolichucky Jack overnight. Tipton feared a riot; and it was decided to send the prisoner for incarceration and trial to Morgantown in North Carolina, just over the hills.

Tipton did not accompany the guards he sent with Sevier. It was stated and commonly believed that he had given instructions of which the honorable men among his friends were ignorant. When the party entered the mountains, two of the guards were to lag behind with the prisoner, till the others were out of sight on the twisting trail. Then one of the two was to kill Sevier and assert that he had done it because Sevier had attempted to escape. It fell out almost as planned, except that the other guard warned Sevier of the fate in store for him and gave him a chance to flee. In plunging down the mountain, Sevier's horse was entangled in a thicket. The would-be murderer overtook him and fired; but here again fate had interposed for her favorite. The ball had dropped out of the assassin's pistol. So Sevier reached Morgantown in safety and was deposited in care of the sheriff, who was doubtless cautioned to take a good look at the prisoner and know him for a dangerous and a daring man.

JAMES ROBERTSON

Portrait by Washington B. Cooper, Nashville. In the collection of the Tennessee Historical Society. Photograph in the collections of Archibald Henderson.

JAMES ROBERTSON

Portrait by Washington B. Cooper, Nashville. In the collection
of the Tennessee Historical Society. Photograph in the collections
of Archibald Henderson.

There is a story to the effect that, when Sevier was arraigned in the courthouse at Morgantown and presently dashed through the door and away on a racer that had been brought up by some of his friends, among those who witnessed the proceedings was a young Ulster Scot named Andrew Jackson; and that on this occasion these two men, later to become foes, first saw each other. Jackson may have been in Morgantown at the time, though this is disputed; but the rest of the tale is pure legend invented by some one whose love of the spectacular led him far from the facts. The facts are less theatrical but much more dramatic. Sevier was not arraigned at all, for no court was sitting in Morgantown at the time.[1] The sheriff to whom he was delivered did not need to look twice at him to know him for a daring man. He had served with him at King's Mountain. He struck off his handcuffs and set him at liberty at once. Perhaps he also notified General Charles McDowell at his home in Quaker Meadows of the presence of a distinguished guest in Burke County, for McDowell and his brother Joseph, another officer of militia, quickly appeared and went on Sevier's bond. Nolichucky Jack was

[1] Statement by John Sevier, Junior, in the Draper MSS., quoted by Turner, *Life of General John Sevier*, p. 182.

presently holding a court of his own in the tavern, with North Carolina's men at arms — as many as were within call — drinking his health. So his sons and a company of his Wataugans found him, when they rode into Morgantown to give evidence in his behalf — with their rifles. Since none now disputed the way with him, Sevier turned homeward with his cavalcade, McDowell and his men accompanying him as far as the pass in the hills.

No further attempt was made to try John Sevier for treason, either west or east of the mountains. In November, however, the Assembly passed the Pardon Act, and thereby granted absolution to every one who had been associated with the State of Franklin, *except John Sevier*. In a clause said to have been introduced by Tipton, now a senator, or suggested by him, John Sevier was debarred forever from "the enjoyment of any office of profit or honor or trust in the State of North Carolina."

The overhill men in Greene County took due note of the Assembly's fiat and at the next election sent Sevier to the North Carolina Senate. Nolichucky Jack, whose demeanor was never so decorous as when the ill-considered actions of those in authority had made him appear to have circumvented the law, considerately waited outside until the House had lifted the ban — which it did perforce and by a large majority, despite Tipton's opposition — and then took his seat on the senatorial bench beside his enemy. The records show that he was reinstated as Brigadier General of the Western Counties and also appointed at the head of the Committee on Indian Affairs.

Not only in the region about Watauga did the pioneers of Tennessee endure the throes of danger and strife during these years. The little settlements on the Cumberland, which were scattered over a short distance of about twenty-five or thirty miles and had a frontier line of two hundred miles, were terribly afflicted. Their nearest white neighbors among the Kentucky settlers were one hundred and fifty miles away; and through the cruelest years these could render no aid — could not, indeed, hold their own stations. The Kentuckians, as we have seen, were bottled up in Harrodsburg and Boonesborough; and, while the northern Indians led by Girty and Dequindre darkened the Bloody Ground anew, the Cumberlanders were making a desperate stand against the Chickasaws and the Creeks. So terrible was their situation that panic took hold on them, and they would have fled but for the influence of Robertson. He may have put the question to them in the biblical words, "Whither shall I flee?" For they were surrounded, and those who did attempt to escape were "weighed on the path and made light." Robertson knew that their only chance of survival was to stand their ground. The greater risks he was willing to take in person, for it was he who made trips to Boonesborough and Harrodsburg for a share of the powder and lead which John Sevier was sending into Kentucky from time to time. In the stress of conflict Robertson bore his full share of grief, for his two elder sons and his brother fell. He himself was often near to death. One day he was cut off in the fields and was shot in the foot as he ran, yet he managed to reach shelter. There is a story that, in an attack during one of his absences, the Indians forced the outer gate of the fort and Mrs. Robertson went out of her cabin, firing, and let loose a band of the savage dogs which the settlers kept for their protection, and so drove out the invaders.

The Chickasaws were loyal to the treaty they had made with the British in the early days of James Adair's association with them. They were friends to England's friends and foes to her foes.

While they resented the new settlements made on land they considered theirs, they signed a peace with Robertson at the conclusion of the War of Independence. They kept their word with him as they had kept it with the British. Furthermore, their chief, Opimingo or the Mountain Leader, gave Robertson his assistance against the Creeks and the Choctaws and, in so far as he understood its workings, informed him of the new Spanish and French conspiracy, which we now come to consider. So once again the Chickasaws were servants of destiny to the English-speaking race, for again they drove the wedge of their honor into an Indian solidarity welded with European gold.

Since it was generally believed at that date that the tribes were instigated to war by the British and supplied by them with their ammunition, savage inroads were expected to cease with the signing of peace. But Indian warfare not only continued; it increased. In the last two years of the Revolution, when the British were driven from the Back Country of the Carolinas and could no longer reach the tribes with consignments of firearms and powder, it should have been evident that the Indians had other sources of supply and other allies, for they lacked nothing which could aid them in their efforts to exterminate the settlers of Tennessee.

Neither France nor Spain wished to see an English-speaking republic based on ideals of democracy successfully established in America. Though in the Revolutionary War, France was a close ally of the Americans and Spain something more than a nominal one, the secret diplomacy of the courts of the Bourbon cousins ill matched with their open professions. Both cousins hated England. The American colonies, smarting under injustice, had offered a field for their revenge. But hatred of England was not the only reason why activities had been set afoot to increase the discord which should finally separate the colonies from Great Britain and leave the destiny of the colonies to be decided by the House of Bourbon. Spain saw in the Americans, with their English modes of thought, a menace to her authority in her own colonies on both the northern and southern continents. This menace would not be stilled but augmented if the colonies should be established as a republic. Such an example might be too readily followed. Though France had, by a secret treaty in 1762, made over to Spain the province of Louisiana, she was not unmindful of the Bourbon motto, "He who attacks

the Crown of one attacks the other." And she saw
her chance to deal a crippling blow at England's
prestige and commerce.

In 1764, the French Minister, Choiseul, had sent
a secret agent, named Pontleroy, to America to assist in making trouble and to watch for any signs
that might be turned to the advantage of *les deux
couronnes*. Evidently Pontleroy's reports were en-
couraging for, in 1768, Johann Kalb — the same
Kalb who fell at Camden in 1780 — arrived in Philadelphia to enlarge the good work. He was not
only, like several of the foreign officers in the War
of Independence, a spy for his Government, but he
was also the special emissary of one Comte de Broglie who, after the colonies had broken with the
mother country, was to put himself at the head of
American affairs. This Broglie had been for years
one of Louis XV's chief agents in subterranean
diplomacy, and it is not to be supposed that he
was going to attempt the stupendous task of
controlling America's destiny without substantial
backing. Spain had been advised meanwhile to
rule her new Louisiana territory with great liber-
ality — in fact, to let it shine as a republic before
the yearning eyes of the oppressed Americans, so
that the English colonists would arise and cast off

their fetters. Once the colonies had freed themselves from England's protecting arm, it would be
a simple matter for the Bourbons to gather them in
like so many little lost chicks from a rainy yard.
The intrigants of autocratic systems have never
been able to understand that the urge of the spirit
of independence in men is not primarily to break
shackles but to *stand alone* and that the breaking
of bonds is incidental to the true demonstration of
freedom. The Bourbons and their agents were no
more nor less blind to the great principle stirring
the hearts of men in their day than were the Prus-
sianized hosts over a hundred years later who, having themselves no acquaintance with the law of
liberty, could not foresee that half a world would
rise in arms to maintain that law.

When the War of Independence had ended, the
French Minister, Vergennes, and the Spanish Minister, Floridablanca, secretly worked in unison to
prevent England's recognition of the new republic;
and Floridablanca in 1782 even offered to assist
England if she would make further efforts to sub-
due her "rebel subjects." Both Latin powers had
their own axes to grind, and America was to tend
the grindstone. France looked for recovery of her
old prestige in Europe and expected to supersede

England in commerce. She would do this, in the beginning, chiefly through control of America and of America's commerce. Vergennes therefore sought not only to dictate the final terms of peace but also to say what the American commissioners should and should not demand. Of the latter gentlemen he said that they possessed "*caractères peu maniables!*" In writing to Luzerne, the French Ambassador in Philadelphia, on October 14, 1782, Vergennes said: "it behooves us to leave them [the American commissioners] to their illusions, to do everything that can make them fancy that we share them, and undertake only to defeat any attempts to which those illusions might carry them if our coöperation is required." Among these "illusions" were America's desires in regard to the fisheries and to the western territory. Concerning the West, Vergennes had written to Luzerne, as early as July 18, 1780: "At the moment when the revolution broke out, the limits of the Thirteen States did not reach the River [Mississippi] and it would be absurd for them to claim the rights of England, a power whose rule they had abjured." By the secret treaty with Spain, furthermore, France had agreed to continue the war until Gibraltar should be taken, and — if the British should be driven from Newfoundland — to share the fisheries only with Spain, and to support Spain in demanding that the Thirteen States renounce all territory west of the Alleghanies. The American States must by no means achieve a genuine independence but must feel the need of sureties, allies, and protection.[1]

So intent was Vergennes on these aims that he sent a secret emissary to England to further them there. This act of his perhaps gave the first inkling to the English statesmen[2] that American and French desires were not identical and hastened England's recognition of American independence and her agreement to American demands in regard to the western territory. When, to his amazement, Vergennes learned that England had acceded to all America's demands, he said that England had "bought the peace" rather than made it. The policy of Vergennes in regard to America was not unjustly pronounced by a later French statesman "*a vile speculation.*"

[1] See John Jay, *On the Peace Negotiations of 1782–1783 as Illustrated by the Secret Correspondence of France and England*, New York, 1888.

[2] "Your Lordship was well founded in your suspicion that the granting of independence to America as a previous measure is a point which the French have by no means at heart and perhaps are entirely averse from." Letter from Fitzherbert to Grantham, September 3, 1782.

Through England's unexpected action, then, the Bourbon cousins had forever lost their opportunity to dominate the young but spent and war-weakened Republic, or to use America as a catspaw to snatch English commerce for France. It was plain, too, that any frank move of the sort would range the English alongside of their American kinsmen. Since American Independence was an accomplished fact and therefore could no longer be prevented, the present object of the Bourbon cousins was to restrict it. The Appalachian Mountains should be the western limits of the new nation. Therefore the settlements in Kentucky and Tennessee must be broken up, or the settlers must be induced to secede from the Union and raise the Spanish banner. The latter alternative was held to be preferable. To bring it about the same methods were to be continued which had been used prior to and during the war — namely, the use of *agents provocateurs* to corrupt the ignorant and incite the lawless, the instigation of Indian massacres to daunt the brave, and the distribution of gold to buy the avaricious.

As her final and supreme means of coercion, Spain refused to America the right of navigation on the Mississippi and so deprived the Westerners of a market for their produce. The Northern States, having no immediate use for the Mississippi, were willing to placate Spain by acknowledging her monopoly of the great waterway. But Virginia and North Carolina were determined that America should not, by congressional enactment, surrender her "natural right"; and they cited the proposed legislation as their reason for refusing to ratify the Constitution. "The act which abandons it [the right of navigation] is an act of separation between the eastern and western country," Jefferson realized at last. "An act of separation" — that point had long been very clear to the Latin sachems of the Mississippi Valley!

Bounded as they were on one side by the precipitous mountains and on the other by the southward flow of the Mississippi and its tributary, the Ohio, the trappers and growers of corn in Kentucky and western Tennessee regarded New Orleans as their logical market, as the wide waters were their natural route. If market and route were to be closed to them, their commercial advancement was something less than a dream.

In 1785, Don Estevan Miró, a gentleman of artful and winning address, became Governor of Louisiana and fountainhead of the propaganda.

He wrote benign and brotherly epistles to James Robertson of the Cumberland and to His Excellency of Franklin, suggesting that to be of service to them was his dearest aim in life; and at the same time he kept the southern Indians continually on the warpath. When Robertson wrote to him of the Creek and Cherokee depredations, with a hint that the Spanish might have some responsibility in the matter, Miró replied by offering the Cumberlander a safe home on Spanish territory with freedom of religion and no taxes. He disclaimed stirring up the Indians. He had, in fact, advised Mr. McGillivray, chief of the Creeks, to make peace. He would try again what he could do with Mr. McGillivray. As to the Cherokees, they resided in a very distant territory and he was not acquainted with them; he might have added that he did not need to be: his friend McGillivray was the potent personality among the Southern tribes.

In Alexander McGillivray, Miró found a weapon fashioned to his hand. If the Creek chieftain's figure might stand as the symbol of treachery, it is none the less one of the most picturesque and pathetic in our early annals. McGillivray, it will be remembered, was the son of Adair's friend Lachlan McGillivray, the trader, and a Creek woman whose sire had been a French officer. A brilliant and beautiful youth, he had given his father a pride in him which is generally denied to the fathers of sons with Indian blood in them. The Highland trader had spared nothing in his son's education and had placed him, after his school days, in the business office of the large trading establishment of which he himself was a member. At about the age of seventeen Alexander had become a chieftain in his mother's nation; and doubtless it is he who appears shortly afterwards in the Colonial Records as the White Leader whose influence is seen to have been at work for friendship between the colonists and the tribes. When the Revolutionary War broke out, Lachlan McGillivray, like many of the old traders who had served British interests so long and so faithfully, held to the British cause. Georgia confiscated all his property and Lachlan fled to Scotland. For this, his son hated the people of Georgia with a perfect hatred. He remembered how often his father's courage alone had stood between those same people and the warlike Creeks. He could recall the few days in 1760 when Lachlan and his fellow trader, Galphin, at the risk of their lives had braved the Creek warriors — already painted for war and on the march — and so had saved the settlements of the Back Country from extermination. He looked upon the men of Georgia as an Indian regards those who forget either a blood gift or a blood vengeance. And he embraced the whole American nation in his hatred for their sakes.

In 1776 Alexander McGillivray was in his early thirties — the exact date of his birth is uncertain.[1] He had, we are told, the tall, sturdy, but spare physique of the Gael, with a countenance of Indian color though not of Indian cast. His overhanging brows made more striking his very large and luminous dark eyes. He bore himself with great dignity; his voice was soft, his manner gentle. He might have been supposed to be some Latin courtier but for the barbaric display of his dress and his ornaments. He possessed extraordinary personal magnetism, and his power extended beyond the Creek nation to the Choctaws and Chickasaws and the Southern Cherokees. He had long been wooed by the Louisiana authorities, but there is no evidence that he had made alliance with them prior to the Revolution.

[1] Probably about 1741 or 1742. Some writers give 1739 and others 1746. His father landed in Charleston, Pickett (*History of Alabama*) says, in 1735, and was then only sixteen.

Early in the war he joined the British, received a colonel's commission, and led his formidable Creeks against the people of Georgia. When the British were driven from the Back Countries, McGillivray, in his British uniform, went on with the war. When the British made peace, McGillivray exchanged his British uniform for a Spanish one and went on with the war. In later days, when he had forced Congress to pay him for his father's confiscated property and had made peace, he wore the uniform of an American Brigadier General; but he did not keep the peace, never having intended to keep it. It was not until he had seen the Spanish plots collapse and had realized that the Americans were to dominate the land, that the White Leader ceased from war and urged the youths of his tribe to adopt American civilization.

Spent from hate and wasted with dissipation, he retired at last to the spot where Lachlan had set up his first Creek home. Here he lived his few remaining days in a house which he built on the site of the old ruined cabin about which still stood the little grove of apple trees his father had planted. He died at the age of fifty of a fever contracted while he was on a business errand in Pensacola. Among those who visited him in his last years, one has left this description of him: "Dissipation has sapped a constitution originally delicate and feeble. He possesses an atticism of diction aided by a liberal education, a great fund of wit and humor meliorated by a perfect good nature and politeness." Set beside that kindly picture this rough etching by James Robertson: "The biggest devil among them [the Spaniards] is the half Spaniard, half Frenchman, half Scotchman and altogether Creek scoundrel, McGillivray."

How indefatigably McGillivray did his work we know from the bloody annals of the years which followed the British-American peace, when the men of the Cumberland and of Franklin were on the defensive continually. How cleverly Miró played his personal rôle we discover in the letters addressed to him by Sevier and Robertson. These letters show that, as far as words go at any rate, the founders of Tennessee were willing to negotiate with Spain. In a letter dated September 12, 1788, Sevier offered himself and his tottering State of Franklin to the Spanish King. This offer may have been made to gain a respite, or it may have been genuine. The situation in the Tennessee settlements was truly desperate, for neither North Carolina nor Congress apparently cared in the least what befell them or how soon. North Carolina indeed was in an anomalous position, as she had not yet ratified the Federal Constitution. If Franklin went out of existence and the territory which it included became again part of North Carolina, Sevier knew that a large part of the newly settled country would, under North Carolina's treaties, revert to the Indians. That meant ruin to large numbers of those who had put their faith in his star, or else it meant renewed conflict either with the Indians or with the parent State. The probabilities are that Sevier hoped to play the Spaniards against the Easterners who, even while denying the Westerners' contention that the mountains were a "natural" barrier between them, were making of them a barrier of indifference. It would seem so, because, although this was the very aim of all Miró's activities so that, had he been assured of the sincerity of the offer, he must have grasped at it, yet nothing definite was done. And Sevier was presently informing Shelby, now in Kentucky, that there was a Spanish plot afoot to seize the western country.

Miró had other agents besides McGillivray — who, by the way, was costing Spain, for his own services and those of four tribes aggregating over six thousand warriors, a sum of fifty-five thousand dollars a year. McGillivray did very well as superintendent of massacres; but the Spaniard required a different type of man, an American who enjoyed his country's trust, to bring the larger plan to fruition. Miró found that man in General James Wilkinson, lately of the Continental Army and now a resident of Kentucky, which territory Wilkinson undertook to deliver to Spain, for a price. In 1787 Wilkinson secretly took the oath of allegiance to Spain and is listed in the files of the Spanish secret service, appropriately, as "Number Thirteen." He was indeed the thirteenth at table, the Judas at the feast. Somewhat under middle height, Wilkinson was handsome, graceful, and remarkably magnetic. Of a good, if rather impoverished, Maryland family, he was well educated and widely read for the times. With a brilliant and versatile intellectuality and ready gifts as a speaker, he swayed men easily. He was a bold soldier and was endowed with physical courage, though when engaged in personal contests he seldom exerted it — preferring the red tongue of slander or the hired assassin's shot from behind cover. His record fails to disclose one commendable trait. He was inordinately avaricious, but love of money was not his whole motive force: he had a spirit so jealous and malignant that he hated to the death another man's good. He seemed to divine instantly wherein other men were weak and to understand the speediest and best means of suborning them to his own interests — or of destroying them.

Wilkinson was able to lure a number of Kentuckians into the separatist movement. George Rogers Clark seriously disturbed the arch plotter by seizing a Spanish trader's store wherewith to pay his soldiers, whom Virginia had omitted to recompense. This act aroused the suspicions of the Spanish, either as to Number Thirteen's perfect loyalty or as to his ability to deliver the western country. In 1786, when Clark led two thousand men against the Ohio Indians in his last and his only unsuccessful campaign, Wilkinson had already settled himself near the Falls (Louisville) and had looked about for mischief which he might do for profit. Whether his influence had anything to do with what amounted virtually to a mutiny among Clark's forces is not ascertainable; but, for a disinterested onlooker, he was overswift to spread the news of Clark's debacle and to declare gleefully that Clark's sun of military glory had now forever set. It is also known that he later served other generals treacherously in Indian expeditions and that he intrigued with Mad Anthony Wayne's Kentucky troops against their commander.

Spain did not wish to see the Indians crushed; and Wilkinson himself both hated and feared any other officer's prestige. How long he had been in foreign pay we can only conjecture, for, several years before he transplanted his activities to Kentucky, he had been one of a cabal against Washington. Not only his ambitions but his nature must inevitably have brought him to the death-battle with George Rogers Clark. As a military leader, Clark had genius, and soldiering was his passion. In nature, he was open, frank, and bold to make foes if he scorned a man's way as ignoble or dishonest. Wilkinson suavely set about scheming for Clark's ruin. His communication or memorial to the Virginia Assembly — signed by himself and a number of his friends — villifying Clark, ended Clark's chances for the commission in the Continental Army which he craved. It was Wilkinson who made public an incriminating letter which had Clark's signature attached and which Clark said he had never seen. It is to be supposed that Number Thirteen was responsible also for the malevolent anonymous letter accusing Clark of drunkenness and scheming which, so strangely, found its way into the Calendar of State Papers of Virginia.[1]   As a result, Clark was censured by Virginia.   Thereupon he petitioned for a Court of Inquiry, but this was not granted.   Wilkinson had to get rid of Clark; for if Clark, with his military gifts and his power over men, had been elevated to a position of command under the smile of the Government, there would have been small opportunity for James Wilkinson to lead the Kentuckians and to gather in Spanish gold.   So the machinations of one of the vilest traitors who ever sold his country were employed to bring about the stultification and hence the downfall of a great servant.

Wilkinson's chief aids were the Irishmen, O'Fallon, Nolan, and Powers.   Through Nolan, he also vended Spanish secrets.   He sold, indeed, whatever and whomever he could get his price for.   So clever was he that he escaped detection, though he was obliged to remove some suspicions.   He succeeded Wayne as commander of the regular army in 1796.   He was one of the commissioners

[1] See Thomas M. Greene's *The Spanish Conspiracy*, p. 72, footnote. It is possible that Wilkinson's intrigues provide data for a new biography of Clark which may recast in some measure the accepted view of Clark at this period.

to receive Louisiana when the Purchase was arranged in 1803. He was still on the Spanish pay roll at that time. Wilkinson's true record came to light only when the Spanish archives were opened to investigators.

There were British agents also in the Old Southwest, for the dissatisfaction of the Western men inspired in Englishmen the hope of recovering the Mississippi Basin. Lord Dorchester, Governor of Canada, wrote to the British Government that he had been approached by important Westerners; but he received advice from England to move slowly. For complicity in the British schemes, William Blount, who was first territorial Governor of Tennessee and later a senator from that State, was expelled from the Senate.

Surely there was never a more elaborate network of plots that came to nothing! The concession to Americans in 1796 of the right of navigation on the Mississippi brought an end to the scheming.

In the same year Tennessee was admitted to the Union, and John Sevier was elected Governor. Sevier's popularity was undiminished, though there were at this time some sixty thousand souls in Tennessee, many of whom were late comers who had not known him in his heyday. His old power to win men to him must have been as strong as ever, for it is recorded that he had only to enter a political meeting — no matter whose — for the crowd to cheer him and shout for him to "give them a talk."

This adulation of Sevier still annoyed a few men who had ambitions of their own. Among these was Andrew Jackson, who had come to Jonesborough in 1788, just after the collapse of the State of Franklin. He was twenty-one at that time, and he is said to have entered Jonesborough riding a fine racer and leading another, with a pack of hunting dogs baying or nosing along after him. A court record dated May 12, 1788, avers that "Andrew Jackson, Esq. came into Court and produced a licence as an Attorney With A Certificate sufficiently Attested of his Taking the Oath Necessary to said office and Was admitted to Practiss as an Attorney in the County Courts." Jackson made no history in old Watauga during that year. Next year he moved to Nashville, and one year later, when the Superior Court was established (1790), he became prosecuting attorney.

The feud between Jackson and Sevier began about the time that Tennessee entered the Union.

Jackson, then twenty-nine, was defeated for the post of Major General of the Militia through the influence which Sevier exercised against him, and it seems that Jackson never forgave this opposition to his ambitions. By the close of Sevier's third term, however, in 1802, when Archibald Roane became Governor, the post of Major General was again vacant. Both Sevier and Jackson offered themselves for it, and Jackson was elected by the deciding vote of the Governor, the military vote having resulted in a tie. A strong current of influence had now set in against Sevier and involved charges against his honor. His old enemy Tipton was still active. The basis of the charges was a file of papers from the entry-taker's office which a friend of Tipton's had laid before the Governor, with an affidavit to the effect that the papers were fraudulent. Both the Governor and Jackson believed the charges. When we consider what system or lack of system of land laws and land entries obtained in Watauga and such primitive communities — when a patch of corn sealed a right and claims were made by notching trees with tomahawks — we may imagine that a file from the land office might appear easily enough to smirch a landholder's integrity. The scandal was, of course,

used in an attempt to ruin Sevier's candidacy for
a fourth term as Governor and to make certain
Roane's reëlection. To this end Jackson bent
all his energies but without success. Nolichucky
Jack was elected, for the fourth time, as Governor
of Tennessee.

Not long after his inauguration, Sevier met Jackson in Knoxville, where Jackson was holding court.
The charges against Sevier were then being made
the subject of legislative investigation instituted
by Tipton, and Jackson had published a letter in
the Knoxville *Gazette* supporting them. At the sight
of Jackson, Sevier flew into a rage, and a fiery
altercation ensued. The two men were only restrained from leaping on each other by the inter-
vention of friends. The next day Jackson sent
Sevier a challenge which Sevier accepted, but with
the stipulation that the duel take place outside the
State. Jackson insisted on fighting in Knoxville,
where the insult had been offered. Sevier refused.
"I have some respect," he wrote, "for the laws of
the State over which I have the honor to preside,
although you, a judge, appear to have none." No
duel followed; but, after some further *billets-doux*,
Jackson published Sevier as "a base coward and
poltroon. He will basely insult but has not the

courage to repair the wound." Again they met, by accident, and Jackson rushed upon Sevier with his cane. Sevier dismounted and drew his pistol but made no move to fire. Jackson, thereupon, also drew his weapon. Once more friends interfered. It is presumable that neither really desired the duel. By killing Nolichucky Jack, Jackson would have ended his own career in Tennessee — if Sevier's tribe of sons had not, by a swifter means, ended it for him. At this date Jackson was thirty-six. Sevier was fifty-eight; and he had seventeen children.

The charges against Sevier, though pressed with all the force that his enemies could bring to bear, came to nothing. He remained the Governor of Tennessee for another six years — the three terms in eight years allowed by the constitution. In 1811 he was sent to Congress for the second time, as he had represented the Territory there twenty years earlier. He was returned again in 1813. At the conclusion of his term in 1815 he went into the Creek country as commissioner to determine the Creek boundaries, and here, far from his Bonnie Kate and his tribe, he died of fever at the age of seventy. His body was buried with full military honors at Tuckabatchee, one of the Creek towns. In 1889, Sevier's remains were removed to Knoxville and a high marble spire was raised above them.

His Indian enemies forgave the chastisement he had inflicted on them and honored him. In times of peace they would come to him frequently for advice. And in his latter days, the chiefs would make state visits to his home on the Nolichucky River. "John Sevier is a good man" — so declared the Cherokee, Old Tassel, making himself the spokesman of history.

Sevier had survived his old friend, co-founder with him of Watauga, by one year. James Robertson had died in 1814 at the age of seventy-two, among the Chickasaws, and his body, like that of his fellow pioneer, was buried in an Indian town and lay there until 1825, when it was removed to Nashville.

What of the red tribes who had fought these great pioneers for the wide land of the Old Southwest and who in the end had received their dust and treasured it with honor in the little soil remaining to them? Always the new boundary lines drew closer in, and the red men's foothold narrowed before the pushing tread of the whites. The day came soon when there was no longer room for

them in the land of their fathers. But far off across
the great river there was a land the white men did
not covet yet. Thither at last the tribes—Cherokee,
Choctaw, Chickasaw, and Creek — took their
way. With wives and children, maids and youths,
the old and the young, with all their goods, their
cattle and horses, in the company of a regiment
of American troops, they — like the white men
who had superseded them — turned westward. In
their faces also was the red color of the west, but
not newly there. From the beginning of their race,
Destiny had painted them with the hue of the brief
hour of the dying sun.

CHAPTER XI

BOONE'S LAST DAYS

ONE spring day in 1799, there might have been observed a great stir through the valley of the Kanawha. With the dawn, men were ahorse, and women, too. Wagons crowded with human freight wheeled over the rough country, and boats, large and small, were afloat on the streams which pour into the Great Kanawha and at length mingle with the Ohio at Point Pleasant, where the battle was fought which opened the gates of Kentucky.

Some of the travelers poured into the little settlement at the junction of the Elk and the Kanawha, where Charleston now lies. Others, who had been later in starting or had come from a greater distance, gathered along the banks of the Kanawha. At last shouts from those stationed farthest up the stream echoed down the valley and told the rest that what they had come out to see was at hand.

Several pirogues drifted into view on the river,

now brightening in the sunshine. In the vessels were men and their families; bales and bundles and pieces of household furnishings, heaped to the gunwale; a few cattle and horses standing patiently. But it was for one man above all that the eager eyes of the settlers were watching, and him they saw clearly as his boat swung by — a tall figure, erect and powerful, his keen friendly blue eyes undimmed and his ruddy face unlined by time, though sixty-five winters had frosted his black hair.

For a decade these settlers had known Daniel Boone, as storekeeper, as surveyor, as guide and soldier. They had eaten of the game he killed and lavishly distributed. And they too — like the folk of Clinch Valley in the year of Dunmore's War — had petitioned Virginia to bestow military rank upon their protector. "Lieutenant Colonel" had been his title among them, by their demand. Once indeed he had represented them in the Virginia Assembly and, for that purpose, trudged to Richmond with rifle and hunting dog. Not interested in the Legislature's proceedings, he left early in the session and tramped home again.

But not even the esteem of friends and neighbors could hold the great hunter when the deer had fled. So Daniel Boone was now on his way westward to

18

Missouri, to a new land of fabled herds and wide spaces, where the hunter's gun might speak its one word with authority and where the soul of a silent and fearless man might find its true abode in Nature's solitude. Waving his last farewells, he floated past the little groups — till their shouts of good will were long silenced, and his fleet swung out upon the Ohio.

As Boone sailed on down the Beautiful River which forms the northern boundary of Kentucky, old friends and newcomers who had only heard his fame rode from far and near to greet and godspeed him on his way. Sometimes he paused for a day with them. Once at least — this was in Cincinnati where he was taking on supplies — some one asked him why, at his age, he was leaving the settled country to dare the frontier once more.

"Too crowded," he answered; "I want more elbow-room!"

Boone settled at the Femme Osage Creek on the Missouri River, twenty-five miles above St. Charles, where the Missouri flows into the Mississippi. There were four other Kentucky families at La Charette, as the French inhabitants called the post, but these were the only Americans. The Spanish authorities granted Boone 840 acres of land, and here Daniel

Gravure Andersen-Lamb Co N.Y.

built the last cabin home he was to erect for himself and his Rebecca.

The region pleased him immensely. The governmental system, for instance, was wholly to his mind. Taxes were infinitesimal. There were no elections, assemblies, or the like. A single magistrate, or Syndic, decided all disputes and made the few regulations and enforced them. There were no land speculators, no dry-mouthed sons of the commercial Tantalus, athirst for profits. Boone used to say that his first years in Missouri were the happiest of his life, with the exception of his first long hunt in Kentucky.

In 1800 he was appointed Syndic of the district of Femme Osage, which office he filled for four years, until Louisiana became American territory. He was held in high esteem as a magistrate because of his just and wise treatment of his flock, who brought him all their small bickerings to settle. He had no use for legal procedure, would not listen to any nice subtleties, saying that he did not care anything at all about the *evidence*, what he wanted was the *truth*. His favorite penalty for offenders was the hickory rod "well laid on." Often he decided that both parties in a suit were equally to blame and chastised them both alike. When in

March, 1804, the American Commissioner received Louisiana for the United States, Delassus, Lieutenant Governor of Upper Louisiana, reporting on the various officials in the territory, wrote of the Femme Osage Syndic: "Mr. Boone, a respectable old man, just and impartial, he has already, since I appointed him, offered his resignation owing to his infirmities. Believing I know his probity, I have induced him to remain, in view of my confidence in him, for the public good."[1]

Daniel, no doubt supposing that a Syndic's rights were inviolable, had neglected to apply to the Governor at New Orleans for a ratification of his grant. He was therefore dispossessed. Not until 1810, and after he had enlisted the Kentucky Legislature in his behalf, did he succeed in inducing Congress to restore his land. The Kentucky Legislature's resolution was adopted because of "the many eminent services rendered by Colonel Boone in exploring and settling the western country, from which great advantages have resulted not only to the State but to the country in general, and that from circumstances over which he had no

---

[1] Thwaites, *Daniel Boone*. To this and other biographies of Boone, cited in the Bibliographical Note at the end of this volume, the author is indebted for the material contained in this chapter.

control he is now reduced to poverty; not having so far as appears an acre of land out of the vast territory he has been a great instrument in peopling." Daniel was seventy-six then; so it was late in the day for him to have his first experience of justice in the matter of land. Perhaps it pleased him, however, to hear that, in confirming his grant, Congress had designated him as "the man who has opened the way for millions of his fellow-men."

The "infirmities" which had caused the good Syndic to seek relief from political cares must have been purely magisterial. The hunter could have been very little affected by them, for as soon as he was freed from his duties Boone took up again the silent challenge of the forest. Usually one or two of his sons or his son-in-law, Flanders Calloway, accompanied him, but sometimes his only companions were an old Indian and his hunting dog. On one of his hunting trips he explored a part of Kansas; and in 1814, when he was eighty, he hunted big game in the Yellowstone where again his heart rejoiced over great herds as in the days of his first lone wanderings in the Blue Grass country. At last, with the proceeds of these expeditions he was able to pay the debts he had left behind in Kentucky thirty years before. The story runs that

Daniel had only fifty cents remaining when all the claims had been settled, but so contented was he to be able to look an honest man in the face that he was in no disposition to murmur over his poverty.

When after a long and happy life his wife died in 1813, Boone lived with one or other of his sons[1] and sometimes with Flanders Calloway. Nathan Boone, with whom Daniel chiefly made his home, built what is said to have been the first stone house in Missouri. Evidently the old pioneer disapproved of stone houses and of the "luxuries" in furnishings which were then becoming possible to the new generation, for one of his biographers speaks of visiting him in a log addition to his son's house; and when Chester Harding, the painter, visited him in 1819 for the purpose of doing his portrait, he found Boone dwelling in a small log cabin in Nathan's yard. When Harding entered, Boone was broiling a venison steak on the end of his ramrod. During the sitting, one day, Harding

[1] Boone's son Nathan won distinction in the War of 1812 and entered the regular army, rising to the rank of Lieutenant Colonel. Daniel Morgan Boone is said to have been the first settler in Kansas (1827). One of Daniel's grandsons, bearing the name of Albert Gallatin Boone, was a pioneer of Colorado and was to the forefront in Rocky Mountain exploration. Another grandson was the scout, Kit Carson, who led Frémont to California.

asked Boone if he had ever been lost in the woods when on his long hunts in the wilderness.

"No, I never got lost," Boone replied reflectively, "but I was *bewildered* once for three days." Though now having reached the age of eighty-five, Daniel was intensely interested in California and was enthusiastic to make the journey thither next spring and so to flee once more from the civilization which had crept westward along his path. The resolute opposition of his sons, however, prevented the attempt.

A few men who sought out Boone in his old age have left us brief accounts of their impressions. Among these was Audubon. "The stature and general appearance of this wanderer of the western forests," the naturalist wrote, "approached the gigantic. His chest was broad, and prominent; his muscular powers displayed themselves in every limb; his countenance gave indication of his great courage, enterprise and perseverance; and, when he spoke, the very motion of his lips brought the impression that whatever he uttered could not be otherwise than strictly true."

Audubon spent a night under Boone's roof. He related afterwards that the old hunter, having removed his hunting shirt, spread his blankets on the floor and lay down there to sleep, saying that he found it more comfortable than a bed. A striking sketch of Boone is contained in a few lines penned by one of his earliest biographers: "He had what phrenologists would have considered a model head — with a forehead peculiarly high, noble and bold, thin compressed lips, a mild clear blue eye, a large and prominent chin and a general expression of countenance in which fearlessness and courage sat enthroned and which told the beholder at a glance what he had been and was formed to be." In criticizing the various portraits of Daniel, the same writer says: "They want the high port and noble daring of his countenance. . . . Never was old age more green, or gray hairs more graceful. His high, calm, bold forehead seemed converted by years into iron."

Although we are indebted to these and other early chroniclers for many details of Boone's life, there was one event which none of his biographers has related; yet we know that it must have taken place. Even the bare indication of it is found only in the narrative of the adventures of two other explorers.

It was in the winter of 1803 that these two men came to Boone's Settlement, as La Charette was now generally called. They had planned to make their winter camp there, for in the spring, when the Missouri rose to the flood, they and their company of frontiersmen were to take their way up that uncharted stream and over plains and mountains in quest of the Pacific Ocean. They were refused permission by the Spanish authorities to camp at Boone's Settlement; so they lay through the winter some forty miles distant on the Illinois side of the Mississippi, across from the mouth of the Missouri. Since the records are silent, we are free to picture as we choose their coming to the settlement during the winter and again in the spring, for we know that they came.

We can imagine, for instance, the stir they made in La Charette on some sparkling day when the frost bit and the crusty snow sent up a dancing haze of diamond points. We can see the friendly French *habitants* staring after the two young leaders and their men — all mere boys, though they were also husky, seasoned frontiersmen — with their bronzed faces of English cast, as in their gayly fringed deerskins they swaggered through the hamlet to pay their respects to the Syndic. We may think of that dignitary as smoking his pipe before his fireplace, perhaps; or making out, in his

fantastic spelling, a record of his primitive court —
for instance, that he had on that day given Pierre
a dozen hickory thwacks, "well laid on," for starting a brawl with Antoine, and had bestowed the
same upon Antoine for continuing the brawl with
Pierre. A knock at the door would bring the ami-
able invitation to enter, and the two young men
would step across his threshold, while their followers crowded about the open door and hailed
the old pathfinder.

One of the two leaders — the dark slender man
with a subtle touch of the dreamer in his resolute
face — was a stranger; but the other, with the more
practical mien and the shock of hair that gave him
the name of Red Head among the tribes, Boone
had known as a lad in Kentucky. To Daniel and
this young visitor the encounter would be a simple
meeting of friends, heightened in pleasure and
interest somewhat, naturally, by the adventure
in prospect. But to us there is something vast
in the thought of Daniel Boone, on his last frontier, grasping the hands of William Clark and
Meriwether Lewis.

As for the rough and hearty mob at the door,
Daniel must have known not a few of them well;
though they had been children in the days when

he and William Clark's brother strove for Kentucky. It seems fitting that the soldiers with this expedition should have come from the garrison at Kaskaskia; since the taking of that fort in 1778 by George Rogers Clark had opened the western way from the boundaries of Kentucky to the Mississippi. And among the young Kentuckians enlisted by William Clark were sons of the sturdy fighters of still an earlier border line, Clinch and Holston Valley men who had adventured under another Lewis at Point Pleasant. Daniel would recognize in these — such as Charles Floyd — the young kinsmen of his old-time comrades whom he had preserved from starvation in the Kentucky wilderness by the kill from his rifle as they made their long march home after Dunmore's War.

In May, Lewis and Clark's pirogues ascended the Missouri and the leaders and men of the expedition spent another day in La Charette. Once again, at least, Daniel was to watch the westward departure of pioneers. In 1811, when the Astorians passed, one of their number pointed to the immobile figure of "an old man on the bank, who, he said, was Daniel Boone."

Sometimes the aged pioneer's mind cast forward

to his last journey, for which his advancing years were preparing him. He wrote on the subject to a sister, in 1816, revealing in a few simple lines that the faith whereby he had crossed, if not more literally removed, mountains was a fixed star, and that he looked ahead fearlessly to the dark trail he must tread by its single gleam. Autumn was tinting the forest and the tang he loved was in the air when the great hunter passed. The date of Boone's death is given as September 26, 1820. He was in his eighty-sixth year. Unburdened by the pangs of disease he went out serenely, by the gentle marches of sleep, into the new country.

The convention for drafting the constitution of Missouri, in session at St. Louis, adjourned for the day, and for twenty days thereafter the members wore crape on their arms as a further mark of respect for the great pioneer. Daniel was laid by Rebecca's side, on the bank of Teugue Creek, about a mile from the Missouri River. In 1845, the Missouri legislators hearkened to oft-repeated pleas from Kentucky and surrendered the remains of the pioneer couple. Their bones lie now in Frankfort, the capital of the once Dark and Bloody Ground, and in 1880 a monument was raised over them.

To us it seems rather that Kentucky itself is

Boone's monument; even as those other great corn States, Illinois and Indiana, are Clark's. There, these two servants unafraid, who sacrificed without measure in the wintry winds of man's ingratitude, are each year memorialized anew; when the earth in summer — the season when the red man slaughtered — lifts up the full grain in the ear, the life-giving corn; and when autumn smiles in golden peace over the stubble fields, where the reaping and binding machines have hummed a nation's harvest song.

BIBLIOGRAPHICAL NOTE

THE RACES AND THEIR MIGRATION

C. A. Hanna, *The Scotch-Irish*, 2 vols. New York, 1902. A very full if somewhat over-enthusiastic study.

H. J. Ford, *The Scotch-Irish in America*. Princeton, 1915. Excellent.

A. G. Spangenberg, Extracts from his Journal of travels in North Carolina, 1752. Publication of the Southern History Association. Vol. I, 1897.

A. B. Faust, *The German Element in the United States*, 2 vols. (1909).

J. P. MacLean, *An Historical Account of the Settlements of Scotch Highlanders in America* (1900).

S. H. Cobb, *The Story of the Palatines* (1897).

N. D. Mereness (editor), *Travels in the American Colonies*. New York, 1916. This collection contains the diary of the Moravian Brethren cited in the first chapter of the present volume.

LIFE IN THE BACK COUNTRY

Joseph Doddridge, *Notes on the Settlements and Indian Wars of the Western Parts of Virginia and Pennsylvania*, from 1763 to 1783. Albany, 1876. An intimate description of the daily life of the early settlers in the Back Country by one of themselves.

287

J. F. D. Smyth, *Tour in the United States of America*, 2 vols. London, 1784. Minute descriptions of the Back Country and interesting pictures of the life of the settlers; biased as to political views by Royalist sympathies.

William H. Foote, *Sketches of North Carolina*, New York, 1846. See Foote also for history of the first Presbyterian ministers in the Back Country. As to political history, inaccurate.

EARLY HISTORY AND EXPLORATION

J. S. Bassett (editor), *The Writings of Colonel William Byrd of Westover*. New York, 1901. A contemporary record of early Virginia.

Thomas Walker, *Journal of an Exploration in the Spring of the Year 1750*. Boston, 1888. The record of his travels by the discoverer of Cumberland Gap.

William M. Darlington (editor), *Christopher Gist's Journals*. Pittsburgh, 1893. Contains Gist's account of his surveys for the Ohio Company, 1750.

C. A. Hanna, *The Wilderness Trail*, 2 vols. New York, 1911. An exhaustive work of research, with full accounts of Croghan and Findlay. See also Croghan's and Johnson's correspondence in vol. VII, New York Colonial Records.

James Adair, *The History of the American Indians*, etc. London, 1775. The personal record of a trader who was one of the earliest explorers of the Alleghanies and of the Mississippi region east of the river; a many-sided work, intensely interesting.

C. W. Alvord, *The Genesis of the Proclamation of 1763*. Reprinted from Canadian Archives Report, 1906. A new and authoritative interpretation. In this connection see also the correspondence between Sir William

Johnson and the Lords of Trade in vol. VII of New York Colonial Records.

Justin Winsor, *The Mississippi Basin. The Struggle in America between England and France.* Cambridge, 1895. Presents the results of exhaustive research and the coördination of facts by an historian of broad intellect and vision.

Colonial and State Records of North Carolina. 30 vols. The chief fountain source of the early history of North Carolina and Tennessee.

W. H. Hoyt, *The Mecklenburg Declaration of Independence.* New York, 1907. This book presents the view generally adopted by historians, that the alleged Declaration of May 20, 1775, is spurious.

Justin Winsor (editor), *Narrative and Critical History of America.* 8 vols. (1884–1889). Also *The Westward Movement.* Cambridge, 1897. Both works of incalculable value to the student.

C. W. Alvord, *The Mississippi Valley in British Politics.* 2 vols. Cleveland, 1917. A profound work of great value to students.

KENTUCKY

R. G. Thwaites and L. P. Kellogg (editors), *Documentary History of Dunmore's War, 1774.* Compiled from the Draper Manuscripts in the library of the Wisconsin Historical Society. Madison, 1905. A collection of interesting and valuable documents with a suggestive introduction.

R. G. Thwaites, *Daniel Boone.* New York, 1902. A short and accurate narrative of Boone's life and adventures compiled from the Draper Manuscripts and from earlier printed biographies.

19

John P. Hale, *Daniel Boone, Some Facts and Incidents not Hitherto Published.* A pamphlet giving an account of Boone in West Virginia. Printed at Wheeling, West Virginia. Undated.

Timothy Flint, *The First White Man of the West or the Life and Exploits of Colonel Dan'l Boone.* Cincinnati, 1854. Valuable only as regards Boone's later years.

John S. C. Abbott, *Daniel Boone, the Pioneer of Kentucky.* New York, 1872. Fairly accurate throughout.

J. M. Peck, *Daniel Boone* (in Sparks, *Library of American Biography.* Boston, 1847).

William Henry Bogart. *Daniel Boone and the Hunters of Kentucky.* New York, 1856.

William Hayden English, *Conquest of the Country Northwest of the River Ohio, 1778–1783, and Life of General George Rogers Clark,* 2 vols. Indianapolis, 1896. An accurate and valuable work for which the author has made painstaking research among printed and unprinted documents. Contains Clark's own account of his campaigns, letters he wrote on public and personal matters, and also letters from contemporaries in defense of his reputation.

Theodore Roosevelt, *The Winning of the West,* 4 vols. New York, 1889–1896. A vigorous and spirited narrative.

TENNESSEE

J. G. M. Ramsey, *The Annals of Tennessee.* Charleston, 1853. John Haywood, *The Civil and Political History of the State of Tennessee.* Nashville, 1891. (Reprint from 1828.) These works, with the North Carolina *Colonial Records,* are the source books of early Tennessee. In statistics, such as numbers of Indians and other foes defeated by Tennessee heroes, not reliable. Incorrect as to causes of Indian wars during the Revolution. On this subject see letters and reports by John and Henry Stuart in North Carolina *Colonial Records*, vol. x; and letters by General Gage and letters and proclamation by General Ethan Allen in American Archives, Fourth Series, vol. ii, and by President Rutledge of South Carolina in North Carolina *Colonial Records*, vol. x. See also Justin Winsor, *The Westward Movement*.

J. Allison, *Dropped Stitches in Tennessee History*. Nashville, 1897. Contains interesting matter relative to Andrew Jackson in his younger days as well as about other striking figures of the time.

F. M. Turner, *The Life of General John Sevier*. New York, 1910. A fairly accurate narrative of events in which Sevier participated, compiled from the *Draper Manuscripts*.

A. W. Putnam, *History of Middle Tennessee, or Life and Times of General James Robertson*. Nashville, 1859. A rambling lengthy narrative containing some interesting material and much that is unreliable. Its worst fault is distortion through sentimentality, and indulgence in the habit of putting the author's rodomontades into the mouths of Robertson and other characters.

J. S. Bassett, *Regulators of North Carolina*, in Report of the American Historical Association, 1894.

L. C. Draper, *King's Mountain and its Heroes*. Cincinnati, 1881. The source book on this event. Contains interesting biographical material about the men engaged in the battle.

French and Spanish Intrigues

Henry Doniol, *Histoire de la participation de la France á l'établissement des États-Unis d'Amérique*, 5 vols.

Paris, 1886–1892. A complete exposition of the French and Spanish policy towards America during the Revolutionary Period.

Manuel Serrano y Sanz, *El brigadier Jaime Wilkinson y sus tratos con España para la independencia del Kentucky, años 1787 á 1797.* Madrid, 1915. A Spanish view of Wilkinson's intrigues with Spain, based on letters and reports in the Spanish *Archives*.

Thomas Marshall Green, *The Spanish Conspiracy.* Cincinnati, 1891. A good local account, from American sources. The best material on this subject is found in Justin Winsor's *The Westward Movement* and *Narrative and Critical History* because there viewed against a broad historical background. See Winsor also for the Latin intrigues in Tennessee. For material on Alexander McGillivray see the American Archives and the Colonial Records of Georgia.

Edward S. Corwin, *French Policy and the American Alliance of 1778.* Princeton, 1916. Deals chiefly with the commercial aspects of French policy and should be read in conjunction with Winsor, Jay, and Fitzmaurice's *Life of William, Earl of Shelburne.* 3 vols. London, 1875.

John Jay, *On the Peace Negotiations of 1782–83 as Illustrated by the Secret Correspondence of France and England.* New York, 1888. A paper read before the American Historical Association, May 23, 1887.

INDEX

Abingdon (Penn.), Boone family at, 25

Adair, James, pioneer trader, 59-74, 158 (note)

Alabama, Creek nation in, 57

Alabama, Fort, French at, 57, 68

Alamance, Battle of the, 104

Allaire, Lieutenant, officer under Ferguson, 200, 213

Allen, General Ethan, tries to enlist Indian aid in Canada, 176 (note)

Alvord, C. W., *The Mississippi Valley in British Politics*, cited, 110 (note), 113 (note)

American Archives, cited, 8 (note), 123 (note), 176 (note)

Anne, Queen, invites Palatines to England, 15

"Apostle, The," Count Zinzendorf, Moravian leader, 16-17

Attakullakulla, Cherokee statesman, 133

Audubon, J. J., and Boone, 279-280

Avery, Waightstill, 162

Baker, John, companion to Boone, 95

Bean (or Been), William, erects first cabin on Watauga River, 159

Beautiful River, 125, 274

Big Bone Lick, Boone finds, 102

Big Turtle, name given Boone by Indians, 145

Black Fish, Shawanoe chief, 145, 146, 147, 148

Bledsoe, Captain Anthony, 121, 125 (note), 149

Blount, William, Governor of Tennessee, 265

Blue Licks (Ky.), 97, 102, 143; battle at, 152

Bluff Hector, nickname for Hector MacNeill, 12

Bogart, W. H., *Daniel Boone and the Hunters of Kentucky*, cited, 135 (note)

Boone, Albert Gallatin, grandson of Daniel, 278 (note)

Boone, Daniel, nationality, 24-25; family, 24-26, 27-28; born (1734), 26; early life, 26-27; journey to North Carolina, 29-30; home on the Yadkin, 48; Findlay and, 52-53, 83, 90, 97, 98, 100, 131-32; in Braddock's campaign, 83; marriage, 90-91; in Virginia, 92; removes to North Carolina, 92; carving on tree, 93; with Waddell's rangers, 93; travels to Florida, 94; first expedition into Kentucky, 95-97; second Kentucky expedition, 97-103; lonely explorations, 101-02; personal characteristics, 105-106; removes family to Powell's Valley, 106-09; part in Dunmore's war, 120-22, 128; and Henderson's venture, 129, 130 (note), 131, 133, 134-36; at Boonesborough, 140-41, 143,

Tryon, William, Governor of
North Carolina, 104, 160
Tuckabatchee, Creek town, Se-
vier buried at, 269
Turner, F. M., *Life of General
John Sevier*, cited, 243 (note)

Ulster Plantation, 3–4
Ulstermen, *see* Scotch-Irish

Vergennes, Charles Gravier,
Comte de, French Minister,
250, 251, 252
Virginia, claim to the Ohio, 76–
77; Indian policy, 83; Indians
apply for redress to, 85; Daniel
Boone in, 92; disputes Fort
Pitt with Pennsylvania, 112;
Harrodsburg Remonstrance,
140; Clark and, 140, 142; and
Boone, 141; and Mississippi
River navigation, 254
Virginia, Valley of, Müller's set-
tlement in, 16

Wachovia Tract, 18
Waddell, Hugh, of North Carolina, in French and Indian
wars, 86, 87; erects fort on
Holston, 158; and Regulation
Movement, 163
Walpole Company, 112
War of 1812, part of mountaineers in, 224
Ward, James, 95
Ward, Nancy, half-caste Cherokee prophetess, 174, 177
Warriors' Path, 107, 132, 134,
186
Washington, George, journeys
to Fort Le Bœuf, 79; at
Great Meadows, 81; "Brad-
dock's Defeat," 82; surveys
in Kentucky, 111; tries to
secure land patents for soldiers, 113; and Indian allies,
176 (note); Ferguson's story
of, 199

Washington, District of, 233
Washington County, erected by
North Carolina, 172; divided,
184
Watauga Colony, lands leased to,
134; Harrod and Logan get
supplies from, 141–42; William Bean builds first cabin,
159; and Regulators, 163;
Robertson at, 165–66, 170,
181; Sevier at, 166–67, 169,
200; found to be on Indian
lands, 170; petitions North
Carolina for annexation, 171–
172; made into Washington
County, 172; Indian attacks
on, 176, 181–83; and King's
Mountain, 200–01, 205; *see also*
Frankland, Franklin, Tennes-
see
Wayne, Mad Anthony, 263
Welsh in America, 54
Wheeling (W. Va.), as rendez-
vous for troops, 115; Cresap
at, 116
White Eyes, Delaware chief,
118
Wilkinson, General James, 261–
265
Williams, Colonel, 209
Williams, Jaret, 173
Winchester, German settlement
near, 16
Winsor, Justin, *The Westward
Movement*, quoted, 176 (note)
Winston, Major, 176 (note)
Woolwich, Ferguson studies at,
197
Wyandot Indians, 114

Yadkin Valley, Scotch-Irish in,
7; Craighead in, 8; High-
landers in, 12–13; Moravians
in, 23; life in, 36, 47; hunting,
43, 105; Boone's home in, 48,
90, 97; Presbyterian ministers
in, 50
Yamasi, Indians, 56; Massacre,
55